Courage to Care

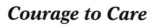

Courage to Care
Helping the Aging, Grieving, and Dying

Jeffrey A. Watson

BAKER BOOK HOUSE
Grand Rapids, Michigan 49516

Copyright 1992 by
Baker Book House Company
P.O. Box 6287
Grand Rapids, MI 49516

Library of Congress Cataloging-in-Publication Data

Watson, Jeffrey A.
    Courage to care : helping the aging, grieving, and dying / Jeffrey
A. Watson.
       p.   cm.
    Includes bibliographical references and index.
    ISBN 0–8010–9715–0
    1. Church work with the aged.   2. Church work with the bereaved.
   3. Church work with the terminally ill.   4. Caring—Religious
aspects—Christianity.   I. Title.
BV4435.W38   1992   91–47537

Printed in the United States of America

Contents

Preface

The Scripture is eloquent in its trilogy of metaphors: "The grass withers . . . the flowers fall . . . but the word of our God stands forever" (Isa. 40:8; see also Ps. 103:14–16; James 1:10–11; 1 Peter 1:24–25). Mankind, like a rolling green meadow, is blanketed by the withering curse of death. This is the truth of Part 1: Biblical Caregiving. Likewise each fragile flower in that fateful meadow will one day bend back to the earth, portraying the mortal destiny of every human being. This is the truth of Part 2: Personal Caregiving. But were it not for the ever enlivening and ever enduring Word of God, we would be helplessly morose. The same God who designed the living/dying cycle on this planet offers a permanent reservoir of hope and life through Jesus Christ as recorded in the Bible. This is the truth woven throughout the fabric of this book.

As we begin a journey together, let me express thanks to colleagues, friends, and mentors who have helped bring us to this starting point: Jim and Jerry Mae Byrd, Dave Epstein, George Harton, Earl McQuay, J. P. Moreland, Dean Nale, John Reed, Bob Roper, Jim Schuppe,

Jeff Thornley, Tim Webster, and Bob Woodburn. Each
has made his or her enduring mark in the colleges, sem-
inaries, and churches where they minister around
North America. Their thoughts echo throughout these
pages.

For any readers who would desire to augment their
journey so that it would include a historical/extra-
biblical inquiry into aging, grief, and death, I have prepared a supplemental monograph. (See Notes for
details.)[1]

Jeffrey A. Watson

Part 1

Biblical Caregiving

Introduction

Imagine yourself standing on the ragged edge of a gaping hole, a hole yawning like a ravenous mouth. The crowd around the edge chatters away as if a would-be curtain were ready to rise on a long-awaited drama.

The place is real: you are standing in the suburbs of Ur in ancient Sumeria. The crowd gathering has come to bid farewell to a wealthy dignitary. Though the departing loved one is not boarding a locomotive at a crowded depot nor waving from the railing of an ocean liner, his well-wishers are sure that his travels are about to begin. Ironically, the departee lies lifelessly in the center of a massive grave.[1]

The Sumerian standing next to you senses your concern and offers reassurance: "Don't worry. He has food, weapons, magic charms, a house full of furniture—everything he'll need for his journey. Besides, he'll have the best choirs and soldiers, cooks and housekeepers among those servants going along with him."

All at once, the crowd turns its attention to a young girl, perhaps twelve or thirteen years of age, hurrying to join her lifeless master in the death pit. Dressed for the occasion in a beautiful white linen robe, she is scolded for being late. After offering quick apologies, she takes her place in the entourage, still holding her jeweled hairpiece in her hands.

Then the ritual begins: magical chants, eerie music, everybody fulfilling his/her role. Stunned, you watch seventy members of the entourage drink from a potion and lie down in the mat-lined pit. With watchers hurling dirt onto the master and his companions, the young girl meets her appointment with death. Buried alive under tons of well-intentioned dirt, this youngster steps into eternity. The household of servants will go with her, she is told. Life will be the same, serving the master in a new place, she rehearses. Darkness and suffocation silence her thunderous heart.

It staggers our sanity to imagine the Christless ignorance of ancient citizens who lived and died without the light of revealed truth. While we concur that there is life beyond the grave, we are sickened by the hellish darkness of pagan superstition. Thus Part 1 will seek to shine the light of biblical truth on the realities of aging, grief, and death.

1

Why Should We Face Aging, Grief, and Death?

Last Rites—the First Time

With my heart thumping, questions were whizzing through my mind. "He can't be serious! The funeral director wants me to lead the *parade?* I've never even done a funeral before, much less a funeral for a man I've never even met! I don't even know what 'the parade' is!"

I had to stop debating with myself for the moment. The early sixties black Cadillac with spaceshiplike fins had landed. Apparently part of my duty as the minister was to go pick up the widow and escort her to the funeral. Staring out the window at an ocean of tenement buildings, I queried: "Well, how do I know which apartment she lives in?" With the pearly smile of a used-car salesman, he shot back, "You'll figure it out, Reverend."

I did too! Using my seminary-tested logic I went in the nearest tenement door. No stairwell lights or last names on the mailboxes. My suburban hunting instincts weren't working. Then there it was: a whole apartment full of women, sitting silently in the darkness.

With a shaky, "Excuse me," I interrupted the pensive quiet. "Is one of you Mrs. Tyrone? I'm here to conduct the funeral." After what seemed like an eternity, one of them pointed, blank facedly, down the hall. As I was introducing myself to the woman sitting on the edge of the bed, she rose slowly to her feet. "Reverend, just let me rinse my mouth one more time." Staggering, she took a whisky flask from her purse and swallowed deeply. Retracing those darkened stairwells, we headed back to the funeral home.

Before I could escort this bereaved stranger into the chapel, the funeral director stopped me with a firm but polite reprimand: "Now, Reverend, we keep the family in here until you do the parade." Grasping for my composure, I asked if I might see him privately. Wanting to disguise my much-veiled ignorance, I asked: "Just how do you folks do your parades around here?" Grinning, he gave me what I needed: "Just get in front of the casket and lead. We'll roll it behind you with the family behind it. Be sure to move with the music!"

As the little pump organ began its soul-like swing, I was rushed to the "head of the parade," muttering to myself. Glancing backward, I could see the whole line moving like a large caterpillar. I had almost caught on to the footwork of our grieving centipede by the time we entered the chapel. The once-silent comforters were now alive with energy. Tears, clapping, singing, and occasional wails made me give in to the mood of the moment, helping me ventilate some of my nervous jitters.

Nearing the front of the room, I whispered to the mortician: "Where is my pulpit?" Seminary had taught me to always minister behind a pulpit. (It's safer that way.) "Tyrone's your pulpit, Reverend. Just stand behind him and let her go!"

Being massively overprepared, I read every verse I knew from the Old and New Testament about death. After my cerebral lecture was finished, I sat down in an overstuffed chair. Moving the spray of flowers off the coffin lid, the funeral director used his little wrench to spring open the top of the simple coffin, giving the crowd the opportunity to file past for one last look.

In deference to the family, relatives didn't have to file past the coffin: the deceased was rolled to them. With the personal farewells over, the undertaker began wrestling with the coffin lid. Every time he'd try to crank it shut with his little wrench, it would spring open suddenly. "Won't work, Joe," he mouthed across the room to his assistant. But with two of them working, one nearly sitting on the side of the casket, the top was finally fastened down before the gallery of amazed mourners.

As the service ended, we began making our way to the cemetery. There we would not be greeted by fresh flowers, green meadows, or crafted headstones. Because of the penury of the family, the naked hole at which all would give their last respects looked more like a construction site. With my finger in the only passage I hadn't read at the funeral home, my plan was simple: read the text, pray, and escort the widow back to winged Cadillac.

As we neared the interment area, the funeral director spoke to me under his breath. "Reverend, what kind of interment do you do?" Dazed by the question, I put my mind into retrieval mode, hoping to remember the day they covered that in seminary. "Well, the regular kind," I spit back, earnestly looking for cues. Shaking his head, he unbuttoned his sports jacket, pointing to numerous vials, bottles, and boxes pinned to the inside. "I mean, do you use water or sand? 'Cause we've got holy water and regular water; we've got white sand, black sand, and gray sand. You can spray it, sprinkle it, or throw it. Whatever!" As fast as a microcomputer, I chose the gray sand, figuring that was more Protestant and middle of the road.

As the small crowd readied itself for the committal, I kept puzzling over my vial of gray sand. Upon finishing my Bible reading, I hesitated before shaking out my gray sand in the sign of the cross—my first and last such sacrament. By the time I had prayed and began escorting the widow back to the car, I was sure that my ministry that day had been an excuse for ill preparation. Bidding farewell and reclaiming his vial, the funeral director flashed me his big smile: "Reverend, I like your style. Let's do it again sometime!"

What Does It All Mean?

My first experience officiating at last rites was humbling. I learned how much I didn't know. Despite fine training in theology, I was a babe in the real world of pastoral ministry. I had been well trained to preach sermons from behind a pulpit, but on that day in Southeast District of Columbia, my role was more than simply being an orator. On that day my role included escorting the widow, leading the "parade," and improvising a credible and biblical message of God's care to the people gathered.

Over the years since that first sad excuse for shepherding, I've been able to learn from many rich experiences and pastoral mentors. I've learned that different cultures, even different families, have their own ways of handling aging, grief, and death. Though I had lived only ten miles from Mr. Tyrone, I knew nothing about leading parades, rolling the farewell casket, and joining into the gospel style of music with its emotionality. I am comfortable to admit now that it is rare for anyone to lead a rite of passage, like a wedding or a funeral, when the rite is cross-cultural and the leader is ignorant of the host culture.

I've learned, too, how difficult it is for us to conduct a funeral for people we don't know, almost like putting words in their mouths. On top of that, my problems were further complicated because I was poorly adjusted to my own mortality and to the ways of God. But my feelings of remoteness on that day were certainly more than matched by the Tyrones' sense that a stranger had entered their private world.

In the years since my first "at bat" in the major leagues, my funeral mistakes by God's grace have become less frequent and far less dramatic. My eyes and ears have become more sensitive to the "Mrs. Tyrones" and the many dysfunctional ways individuals and families try to cope with their pain. More importantly the Master Teacher has taught me from his Word about how to be "the fragrance of life" to those who are suffering (2 Cor. 2:16).

It may seem arrogant for somebody who didn't even know what "the parade" was to write a book like this. But I am convinced that caring people involved in spiritual ministry must first of all exercise courage to face their own inadequacies as caregivers. Then they must commit themselves to developing and enriching their caregiving skills if their competency would ever approach God's potential for them. My prayer is that you will have a courageous hunger, as I do, for competency to care in the power of Christ.

At the outset of this study we must answer two foundational questions: Why is this book needed, and how should it be read? This has been written to help caregivers knowledgeably and skillfully reach out to those touched by aging, grief, and death. It was undertaken for several strategic reasons.

Why Get Involved?

Anyone even casually familiar with the Bible understands its intense realism about life and its direct approach to confronting human problems. For those of us who live between the poisoned paradise and the lifted curse, we are commanded to care. From the opening pages of Genesis with its Edenic obituary to the prophetic climax of God wiping away all tears, we have a Book about no-nonsense realities.

When you minister as a spiritual caregiver, you are doing the work of the Lord. The God of love delights to reach down from heaven, reaching through you with his everlasting arms to embrace a hurting world. Even if you aren't currently serving in a spiritual caregiver role, your vision for the future is a part of God's good work on the earth. The biblical priorities laid out in this book are for all spiritual caregivers: pastors, elders, deacons, counselors, missionaries, chaplains, teachers, nurses, visitation leaders, doctors, good friends, and caring family members.

Out of the thousands of biblical teachings on aging, grief, and death, a few may crystallize our thinking. Solomon challenges our apathy when he shows us how deeply God cares about those who are nearing death (Prov. 24:10–12). Drawing on Solomon's sentiments, we could picture death as a cliff and sense the tenderness of God toward those near the edge. God becomes super-actively attentive to them because of their heightened opportunity to quest for spiritual truth. Some of those who seem to be obvious sufferers in the spotlight of God's compassion are:

People who are chronically or terminally ill

People living with suicidal thoughts, plans, or previous attempts

People brought near to death through accidents, war, or crime

People who are clinically depressed

People with permanent physical, emotional, or cognitive handicaps

People with chronic pain

People with severe aging-related changes

People grieving the loss of their miscarried, stillborn, aborted, or nonexistent child

People dying of starvation and drought

People held in satanic bondage to the fear of death

People who attend the daily needs of others near the edge of death

People living with death threats for their faith

People on the broad way to destruction: hell

Solomon furthermore reminds us that God constantly monitors how we respond to people near the edge (Prov. 24:10–12). If we don't try, God sees our strength as small. If we rationalize not doing what we are capable of doing, he reveals our selfish motives. If we choose not to be his agent of grace, we bear the consequences of not being in his will. After all, since God had courage to care for us in our sin, he would have us duplicate his compassion to those who are lost in their sin or who are suffering the painful consequences of original sin.

Having courage to care doesn't merely benefit those near the edge of death; it also benefits the rest of us who march steadily toward that same cliff. With this common benefit in view, Moses, an elderly, wisdom-filled man, begged the eternal God to give all his people a sense of their own mortality (Ps. 90:1–2, 12). May God give us the same realism about our numbered days, even as Jesus pledged himself to invest wisely the number of days budgeted to him (John 9:4).

Not surprisingly, congregational leaders in both the Old Testament and New Testament eras upheld the same caregiving priorities. Moses commanded his wilderness congregation to publicly demonstrate their reverence for God by honoring their seniors (Lev. 19:32). The words of the fifth commandment, often quoted to children, were historically spoken to adults (Exod. 20:12). As the Hebrew nation exited Egypt, Moses' words had particular relevance to young and middle adults about how they treated their elderly parents. One can only imagine the challenge of honoring elderly mothers and fathers during a forty-year trek in the blistering desert. But the promise to those who succeeded in this marathon of honor was one of enhanced life—perhaps prolonged, certainly blessed life—in the abundant land of Canaan.

In Jesus' teaching on the family, he builds on the intergenerational laws of Moses (Mark 7:9–13). He soundly reprimands anyone who creates personal standards that allegedly transcend the timeless law of honoring elderly parents. Apparently in Jesus' day, the fundraising committee of the Jerusalem temple talked their worshipers into leaving large portions of their earthly estates to endow the temple. In the event of an untimely death or if a dependent mom and dad had need of special help, the money went to the temple anyway. Jesus' point was simple: If it's God's money, then use it as God would use it: to honor elderly parents.

Paul built on these earlier principles as well when he described the spiritual family of the church (1 Tim. 5:1–3, 8). The very interactional style in the body of

Christ was to model healthy family relationships. In the event that elderly people in the church could not care for themselves, family was to intervene. Faith demanded action, even if it demanded that the congregation become a surrogate caregiving network.

Even if guidance from the Word of God were mute on aging, grief, and death, life experience would indicate that we need courage to care. For instance, a survey of residents at the United States Naval Home in Philadelphia highlighted two key human needs among its population.[1]

Anxiety/Concerns About Dying	60 percent of the residents
Distress in Family Relationships	38 percent of the residents

Simply listening to these hundreds of residents should tell us that more than half of them are worried about dying. Some, no doubt, are anxious about the process of dying: *When will death come? Where? Of what causes? Will there be pain? Will I be alone?* Others, perhaps, are concerned about their spirituality: *Is there life after death? Can I be assured of heaven? Have I lived a good life? Am I prepared to die? Do I have any unfinished business? What are my regrets? Are heaven and hell real? What about purgatory? Reincarnation? What happens if I have unconfessed sin at the time I die? Have I committed the unpardonable sin? What if I have doubts about my faith? What if I haven't been able to get to church for a long time or send offerings; does that hurt my chances with God? Who will do my funeral? Should I be cremated? How will I be remembered? What has my life been worth? What if I had never lived?* Thankfully,

Nicodemus's question reaffirms that men and women can be born again, even when they are old (John 3:4).

This survey also indicated that more than one-third of the residents were distressed about family relationships: interpersonal conflicts, hostility, neglect, and divorce. And other residents struggled with meaninglessness in life, alcohol, sexuality, and financial worries. Anyone with sensitivity to these vast human needs sees myriad opportunities to practice courage to care within institutions, the likes of which abound in greater number every day with the graying of America.

Various trends in American society also suggest the need to have courage to care. Within our culture, there are lifestyle fads which need to be balanced as well as heresies which need to be corrected.

The Rigid Controller.[2] He or she admits to some destinies on the human horizon, destinies like aging, retirement, and death. But this person has an exaggerated sense of power, the power to control his/her own destiny. Through personal discipline and self-assured ingenuity, the Rigid Controller intends to beat the odds. By accumulating wealth, obsessing on physical fitness, or having the optimum health care and retirement program on board, the Rigid Controller plays the role of self-made king. This proud approach to life is roundly criticized by James, the half-brother of our Lord (James 4:13–5:6).

The Deaf Ignorer. Similarly Peter critiques the lifestyle of the Deaf Ignorer (2 Peter 3:13–18). If the Rigid Controller were pictured marching stridently into the future, fists clenched and hands held high, the Deaf Ignorer strolls lazily into the future, backward. Trying to deny what's on the horizon, the Deaf Ignorer lives for today's pleasures, reciting his characteristic motto: "Eat, drink, and be merry."

As corollaries to these cultural fads numerous heresies abound. For instance some Rigid Controllers advocate religious dogmatism as their way of guaranteeing their eternal destinies: Join the right ecclesiastical group and rely on its sacraments.

The secular version of this lifestyle is a hollow scientism, a worldview that manifests itself in an ardent belief that the supernatural does not exist and that modern technology should be able to control the hardships of life. This dominant belief system can produce an irrational insistence on artificially prolonging the dying process through elaborate and expensive medical equipment.

Such an over-reliance on medical technology can help explain why America has become so death denying. At the turn of the century typical Americans lived to be forty-seven years old, experienced the death of a sibling or parent before leaving home, and died in their own homes under the care of relatives by whom they were buried.[3] Now, the average American lives to be seventy-six, reaching middle-age before experiencing any major bereavements, and dies in an institution under the care of professionals who then hand off the corpse to other professionals for burial.

There also are heresies correlated to the lifestyle of the Deaf Ignorer. After all, if the Deaf Ignorer strolls aimlessly backward toward destiny, certain religious tenets more typical of Eastern religion could be appealing, tenets such as:

There is no absolute authority for truth; everything is relative.

Spiritual guidance comes from astral guides, seances, intuition, remembering former lives, and the Tibetan Book of the Dead.

Life is not a one-time stewardship; we are reincar-
nated many times.

Biblical teaching about a two-way judgment is
wrong; near-death and out-of-body experiences
teach more accurately about afterlife.

Parapsychology and the paranormal are marvelous
illustrations of our own innate powers.

While psychic mysticism, like that described above,
rejects the natural laws of physics, narrow scientism
rejects the truths of metaphysics.

Where Is All of This Leading?

The shallowness in each of these cultural fads and
heresies has left American society groping for sound
answers. Thus the number of new studies on death each
year has increased about three hundredfold since 1900,
most in the last twenty years.[4] Similarly, the 668 rec-
ommendations made by the 1981 White House Conference on Aging have barely begun to be implemented
a decade later.[5]

Christians need courage to care so that they can
maintain the balanced lifestyle of the responsible pilgrim (Phil. 3:20–21; Heb. 11:1–12:2). Such a "by-faith"
lifestyle, drawing on truths from the physical and meta-
physical realm, allows us to make responsible plans for
the future with a God-pleasing humility. It allows us to
live with an honest mix of pain and pleasure as we
await the return, judgment, and kingdom of Christ. Ultimately equipped with the Word of God and a realistic
caring model, we are prepared to begin responding to
the mountain of human needs throughout our society.

In addition to the motivations from biblical theology, human need, and American society, most caregivers

feel inadequate and in need of God's help to develop their courage to care. Pastors struggle with the walk-on-water syndrome, churches slip into their own form of age prejudice, and family caregivers battle with burnout. If churches are going to change, then pastors must change. And if family caregivers are going to survive, they will need strategic support. No doubt the requisite solutions must include excellent Bible-based death education, an increased used of lay caregiving systems, and an acute dependence on the Lord.[6]

A friendly warning is in order: The longer we dwell on the tender realities of life and death, the more aware we become of our own unfinished business. Our inability to cure people in our partnership of pain can create a temporary, mild rise in anxiety. But anchoring our ministry in the sufficiency of God (2 Cor. 3:5), we can continue learning and supporting one another, anticipating that this earlier anxiety will resolve into greater understanding, care, and skill.[7]

Guidelines for Caregivers

Two principles are important for caregivers to keep in mind. First, the Bible is the only basis for an enduring courage to care. And second, we should be flexible in practicing our role as spiritual caregivers.

If we purposed to be intensive caregivers but lacked the assurances of biblical truth, we could easily become casualties of our own goodwill. The piercing questions of suffering people would haunt us. A tolerance for empty answers would wear thin, inevitably casting a shadow on our relationship with the dying. Thus we will unashamedly affirm what the Bible teaches about spiritual caregiving for those touched by aging, grief, and death. In the first part, we will lay a theological foundation, looking at the whole of humankind as though it were a meadow of withering grass. In the second part, we will explore how individuals cope as they near the doorway to eternity, looking at each person as a unique, fading flower. Throughout, we'll include the ministerial "how-to" in communicating the Word of God, rooting our strategy in God's eloquent trilogy of metaphors: "The grass withers . . . the flowers fall . . . but the word of our God stands forever" (Isa. 40:8; see also Ps. 103:14–16; James 1:10–11; 1 Peter 1:24–25).

Because we desire to speak the truth in love (Eph. 4:15; 2 Tim. 4:2), we will respectfully integrate biblical teaching with objective research about those to whom we will minister, those in need of our love. For instance, while the Bible tells us that there is a fear of death (Heb. 2:15), interviews have helped us know what particular things people fear. While Paul affirms that we do not mourn hopelessly (1 Thess. 4:13), therapists have clarified the difference between healthy and pathological grief. Just as we infer from the Bible that self-murder is sin, psychological autopsies have helped us discover who is most "at-risk" for suicide. Even as Solomon describes the downward trajectory of acute old age (Eccles. 12:1–7), educational gerontologists have proven that crystallized intelligence (wisdom) remains high while fluid intelligence and sensory capacities decrease with age. Every good gift, whether it be a gift of biblical truth or honest research, is from God.

In addition to a strong confidence in the Word of God, one should also have open-mindedness on the role of spiritual caregivers. If one were to expect this book to be a rigid manual for the clergy robot, it would be a disappointment. We understand that spiritual caregivers come in all shapes and sizes: male and female, old and young, clergy and lay, clinical and nonclinical, outgoing and nonoutgoing, some with public gifts and some with private. So along with the "how-to" emphasis, we will also consider other practical aspects of the ministry.

Ministry Skills	How do we serve those touched by aging, grief, and death?
Theology	Whom do we serve? How did Christ serve?
Motivations	Why do we want to serve?
Objectives	Which primary needs do we target?
Stewardship	How can we stay psychospiritually fit to continue this kind of service?
Growth	How can I (and my congregation) narrow the gap between where we are today and where we want to be tomorrow?

If we are truly open-minded about our role as spiritual caregivers, we will guard against stereotyping ourselves as having it all together. Likewise we will also be flexible in how we view the people we hope to help. Chronological age will probably be the worst way—a stereotyping way—to classify people as being in need. For instance there are seventy-five-year-old retirees who play golf every day and are healthier than most of the people reading this. Just as truly, there are fifty-nine-year-old former executives, bedridden with brain atrophy, dementia, and psychotic depression. What do the thirty-three-year-old pastor following his second kidney transplant, the depressed person musing about "ending it all," the housewife too petrified to go outside of her house, and the seven-year-old on chemotherapy all have in common? They are all people in need. But their needs are as varied as their individual circumstances and their coping repertoire.

Unless we are careful, churches can stereotype inactive senior citizens as if they were less earnest spiritually. Whether their pastors know it or not, the very opposite is often true: interest in spiritual matters is growing for them. While their formal participation at church is probably falling off, their prayer and Bible reading is dramatically improving.[8] We could fall into the trap of looking on the outward appearance and completely ignoring the realm of the heart. In fact, church conferences on aging can abound with accolades about the elderly while hypocritically not including one senior in any part of leadership at the conference. Ultimately the well-balanced caregiver will be ministering to each person, *as an individual,* exploring these kinds of concerns, regardless of the person's age.

Experience	What is happening or has happened to you?
Perceptions	How do you view what is happening or has happened to you?
Behavior	What choices have you made or not made to help yourself in this situation?
Intervention	What could we do together that might truly help you?

I have been learning that it takes maturity to be an effective caregiver. About ten years ago I developed all the warning signals of serious heart trouble. Eventually, the symptoms would be diagnosed as nonorganic. More painfully I would discover that I was serving an idol: the need to please people at any cost, a slavery which I lived out through work addiction. Life was not my problem; but how I was going about life *was* a problem. My obsession with a "to do" list and my inability to say *no* was going to kill me. It took a while to see how obviously my lifestyle was hurting me and others. I lived with the messiah complex, feeling a need to fix people and take total responsibility for them, even if they didn't want my help. I had put myself into unrealistic scenarios many times, including at the Tyrone funeral. Despite what I said, my life shouted: "Ministry is what you do, not who you are." I was a rigid controller who thought he could purge away his feelings of inadequacy by hyperactive duty. Ultimately I saw how chronic stress overload makes us resent the very people we want to help. Each new crisis threatened to become the straw that broke the camel's back. In time the caregiver who started out tender had become demanding and emotionally flat.

If you and I are to truly be a fragrance of life to hurting people, we will need courage to care: to care about God, and neighbor, and self in a biblically wholesome way. If we propose not to grow weary, we will need to count the cost of intense caregiving. We will need to select wisely the needs we tackle. At times we will need to come apart and rest a while, learning to let people love us and take care of us. We will need to be secure, not in our own performance, but in the beloved one who makes us acceptable. By God's grace we will have the heart of Mary and the hands of Martha. And in Reinhold Niebuhr's spirit of caregiving, we'll depend on God to give us the contentment to accept the things we cannot change, the courage to change the things we can, and the wisdom to know the difference.

Discussion Questions

1. As you read about the Tyrone funeral, what thoughts and feelings did you have? How do you imagine you might have responded in the same

situation? Have you had any similar learning experiences, whether as the caregiver or the care recipient? What "do's" and "don'ts" would you advise?

2. When you read Proverbs 24:10–12, how do you keep from being a heroic rescuer, plunging in with the messiah complex, even when people haven't asked for help?

3. Would you add any other kinds of human experiences to the list of those "near the edge"? Which ones? Why?

4. Can you describe some specific ways that families or churches can improve their responsiveness to hurting people? To the elderly?

5. What experiences have you had with patients or in your own life that motivate you to reach out to others?

6. When you think about trends in American society, can you add to the list of subjects which beckon for us to have a courage to care? Illustrate some of the ideas on lifestyles or heresies.

7. Do you tend toward the rigid controller or the deaf ignorer? Please illustrate. Why is this your tendency?

8. If you begin to feel uneasy about the heaviness of reading this book, how will you handle it?

9. What value do you see in including some information in this book that is not taken directly from the Bible?

10. Have you ever stereotyped yourself as the caregiver? Stereotyped others to whom you give care? Please explain.

2

How the Old Testament Helps Us Face Aging, Grief, and Death

Val's world teemed with Australia's most exotic wildlife, renewing her romance with nature.[1] The four-day wilderness trips reconnected the environmentalist to the ultimate truths of her universe.

The park ranger trailer became base camp for the science enthusiast, allowing Val to search the remote areas of the swamp by canoe. She had been warned of the one danger on the horizon: the strong current of the river's mainstream. After a day of spectacular bird watching, Val's second outing opened with a canoe ride into a fine mist which soon gave way to dread. Driven by a menacing wind, water poured from the sky, forcing Val to bail and paddle as she hurried back toward camp.

As Val recrossed the large bend in the waterway, she tried steering around a large piece of driftwood in her path. But strangely some current seemed to be intently moving the log to intercept her canoe. Bursting from her silence, Val identified her opponent: "Yellow eyes? It's a big saltwater crocodile!"

Like a wartime torpedo, the swampy Goliath began ramming the canoe. With instant panic, Val paddled madly, hoping to reach a muddy bank with a tree atop its steep ridge.

As Val's canoe touched land, she stood up to survey her options with the silent enemy lying parallel to the canoe, blazing its yellow eyes at her. Unable to frighten off the creature, Val watched as the unblinking stare turned into a sudden humping of the back: the attack was starting!

Springing from the opposite side of the boat, Val began clawing herself up the slippery embankment as the crocodile burst from the water. Like the sound of biting into a fresh apple, Val's attacker crashed its jaws around her waist.

Instinctively the predator lunged backward, taking its prey like a rag doll, deep under water. Trying to exhaust and disorient its victim, the crocodile took Val into a series of death rolls. By the time the fateful tumbling stopped, the creature began holding Val under water to drown her.

Desperate to breathe, Val was astonished to realize she could crane her neck enough to break the surface of the water. Further amazed, she grabbed a low hanging branch and pulled with all of the energy her fright could muster. Surprised that its prey was still alive, the crocodile relaxed its hold to secure a better bite. But with the jaws opening momentarily, Val yanked herself along the branch, escaping the jaws and coming to rest at the base of the tree.

In seconds another blur of water turned into flashing teeth, crushing across Val's left thigh. Back into the death rolls again, the animal was growling in its throat this time. Groping for the creature's eyes, Val thrust her fingers deep into the sockets, finding nostrils instead. "Dear God, let it finish me off quickly!" she prayed.

As the rolls ended, Val's arm touched a branch once more. Again, pulling with superhuman strength, Val felt the vise unlock. Quickly dragging herself to the base of a tree, Val hid behind it, sitting deathly still. In time Val felt safe enough to begin tending her wounds. With a large portion of her left thigh hanging away from her body, she used her shirt as a tourniquet.

Feeling the nausea of shock, Val tried walking, then crawling. As the rain poured, her leg burned and the swamp spun dizzily before her eyes. Imagining that the swamp would flood, she fumed: "What a cruel joke, to survive a crocodile attack and then to die in the mud!"

Through sheer concentration, Val was able to move herself to an exposed bit of land as darkness fell. Delirious but hopeful, Val lay alone and vulnerable until searching rangers discovered her. After surgeries and skin grafts, Val continued to battle the near-fatal bacteria raging within her, a bacteria contracted either from the crocodile's teeth or the swamp mud.

Years later, despite the major scars and muscle problems in her brutalized leg, Val would be able to walk. Although regular flashbacks would escort her to the scene of the attack, she would learn to face the fears without being controlled by them.

Eden, the Beautiful . . . Eden, the Bizarre

Like Val the original man found his idyllic world one of lush beauty, a shrine of nature's greatest potentials. But also like Val, man was alone. Though his first days could be contently filled with farming the ground, naming the animals, and communing with God, his aloneness would prevent him from populating his majestic world.

Once God created woman, the new couple could pon-
der together the ultimate truths of their universe. Unfortunately, they, like Val, would become aware of dangers
lurking just out of view. Though the Lord had clearly
warned humankind's original parents not to eat from a
certain tree, they would be intercepted by the Evil One,
quickly failing to honor the most basic law of nature:
obedience to God. Seduced by the subtle reptile, Adam
and Eve suffered permanent damage from their first
attack when they left their canoe of obedience.

In the clutches of sin, this once-ideal couple must also
have felt like dying. They, like Val, were far separated
from their safe home. Hiding behind the bushes, they
remembered the words: "You will surely die" (Gen. 2:17).
Though they didn't know how and when they would die,
it must have seemed like Val's cruel joke, to survive a
face-to-face reptilian assault only to die later of lesser
causes in the bacterial mud of a dying humanity.

As spiritual darkness fell, God came like a searching
ranger. Adam and Eve would get a second chance, not to
return to an idyllic world without scars, but to survive to
another day. Like Val's tourniquet, God wrapped his
wounded children in the warm skins of freshly slain animals (3:21). As God sacrificed a substitutionary animal,
he not only provided a wardrobe for this frightened couple; he showed them the wages of sin (Rom. 6:23).

Adam and Eve now had a fatal infection that would
someday claim their physical lives. Despite the bad news,
however, the woman's Seed would one day overcome the
serpent's (Gen. 3:15; Rom. 16:20; John 11:25–26).

No matter how frightening the Edenic flashbacks
might be, humankind needn't be controlled by satanic
fear. Jesus, who conquers the fear of death, holds the
keys to life and death in the cosmic swamp (Heb.
2:14–15; Rev. 1:18). He alone can teach us the realities of

this swamp and how to cope with them. These, then, become our two purposes for this chapter. First to learn the realities of aging, grief, and death in the Old Testament culture. And second to learn how Old Testament believers coped with these stark realities in their day.

Principles of Reality and Survival

Like Val's swamp and Adam's Eden, the world in which we live is poisoned with the smell of death. However rather than becoming morbid about the realities of our world, we can learn survival principles that look to hope beyond the darkness. We can develop a night vision that allows us to live in the shadows skillfully, while we await the eventual sunrise. Val learned not to abandon her canoe as Adam learned not to put personal pleasure and rationalization above obedience to God's Word. Through that same Word, we can learn these principles of reality and survival in the accursed swamp of aging, grief, and death:

> God created the human being as a physical/
> psychospiritual whole.
> God instituted death as the divine judgment on sin.
> God controls the living/dying process now.

Man is a Physical/Psychospiritual Whole

Moses' description of the origin of humanity is simple and accurate (Gen. 2:7). The Creator scooped up rich topsoil and fashioned a handsome mud doll. With the skill of the finest potter, God designed Adam's body, then infused him with life. Adam became more than a corpse with a temporary surge of oxygen into his lungs. He became a living person who could pass on the life principle to his offspring. Clearly then, through this anthropomorphic picture, we learn that the first human was comprised not only of basic earthly material but of an invisible spiritual dynamic as well.

A living soul? A dead soul? Unfortunately, interpreters have wrestled with a phrase in the traditional King James Version translation of Gen. 2:7: "Man became a living soul [Heb. *nepeš*]." To some, this phrase has implied that Adam had previously been a dead soul, a concept that generated numerous questions. Did man have an eternally preexistent soul? Did that soul lie dormant in God's heavenly reservoir of souls until it was implanted into a physical body at conception? Could man's soul become dead again through sin? Did Adam's sin kill the souls of his offspring so that they would be born spiritually dead until they were regenerated by the gospel? Could hell be the final resting place of dead souls?

To cut through some of the theological guesswork, we need to look closely at the way *nepeš* is used in the Old Testament.[2] In the Pentateuch (Lev. 21:11; Num. 6:6), the high priest and Nazirite were forbidden to touch dead people [*nepeš*]. The concept of hygienic and ceremonial uncleanness prevented these leaders from becoming inadvertent carriers of infectious disease, perhaps spreading a contagion to their myriad ministry contacts. This preventive strategy was so strict that men who served as high priests or Nazirites were forbidden to embrace the dead bodies of loved ones.

When we look further into the Old Testament, we see many occasions when *nepeš* is simply a substitute word for the person in general, referring to the whole of his life (Gen. 12:13; Lev. 5:4; 1 Sam. 18:1; 1 Kings 19:4). Nowhere in these passages can a Greek dualism of body vs. soul be sustained.

In general the early Old Testament describes the person as a simple, unitary whole. While this description does not contradict later illumination (Matt. 10:28; 1 Thess. 5:23), it does provide room for the progress of revelation. It furthermore understands that the two primary aspects of the human being are the body (that which God sculpted) and the invisible self (that which God breathed in). Thus, it would be unwise for us to read into any early Old Testament descriptions an over-separation of physical and psychospiritual components. These components are viewed together as is the color, juiciness, and weight of a grape.

What about the breath? In the original account (Gen. 2:7), God is pictured as providing a mouth-to-mouth jump start for the most advanced creature. Because of this narrative and because breathing has long been the most commonly recognized vital sign, other passages also bear on the respiratory spirit (Job 34:14–15; Pss. 104:29–30; 146:4; Eccles. 3:19–21; 12:7).

Since Old Testament saints were not privy to the Harvard Brain Death Criteria nor sophisticated cardio-pulmonary phenomena, the respiratory dynamic represents the vital sign in their day. Theologically these inspired saints understood that God actively provides the very breath of life for his creatures, leaving people radically dependent on him. When, for whatever reason, God stops providing the life breath for a person, the body dies immediately and begins an organic decay back into the natural elements.

Accordingly when man takes his last breath, he dies. Life is simply understood as ending, without comment about an afterlife. In fact from the language of appearance, a dead man can no longer think. Thus he is not perceived to have an ongoing conscious life in another dimension. In fact a philosophy of cynicism might have

said that respiratory failure signals the end for all creatures, human and animal alike. Certainly the skeptic
would argue that humans and animals share two things
in common: the need to breathe and the organic decay
trajectory that begins upon the moment of respiratory
arrest.

By using the test of natural observation, it was and is
impossible to prove any unique destiny for the immaterial aspect of man upon death. And though the
Preacher's wisdom would posit that God retrieves his
spirit/breath dynamic upon man's death, this dynamic
may not have been perceived by some Old Testament
saints as retaining its individual identity.

Life beyond the grave? It is possible that some Old
Testament believers were genuinely ignorant of life
beyond the grave. They may have held notions similar
to modern folk who say "Gesundheit" or "God bless
you!" when someone sneezes. Such a custom is rooted
in the outmoded idea that the very breath which is
sneezed out in such force is the human spirit, briefly
dislodged. Such a sudden out-of-body experience
required God's protective intervention, lest Satan take
split-second advantage of a potential residence.

Perhaps we would do well to remember our own
gradual awakening to the realities of human sexuality—the "birds and the bees." Up through kinder-
garten my best friend was a girl. By the end of elemen-
tary school, girls were strange. And by the end of high
school, there was nothing more exciting than the opposite sex. Certainly the realities of gender, sexuality, and
human reproduction did not change over those eighteen years. What changed was my own maturity and
my ability to assimilate timeless truths so that they
could correct and build on my previous perceptions.
By analogy, the mainstream of early Old Testament

thought was largely unillumined on the tripartite anthropology and individual eschatology of the New Testament. Life and death were basically viewed with a simple holism. Respiratory arrest signaled the end of man's life and the start of organic decay. Although everyone from Adam onward has experienced a conscious, intermediate, and immaterial existence upon death, and though they do stand ready for resurrection, they likely only saw through a glass darkly those things that we have now come to boldly expect.

Death: Divine Judgment on Sin

The direct reading of the Genesis account implies that humans were highly competent but potentially mortal. After God created Adam's body and infused it with life (Gen. 1:27; 2:7), humankind was commissioned to act as the Creator's vice-regent over the earth (1:26–29). But even as Adam began the highly ordered work of classifying the animals and cultivating Eden (2:15, 19–20), he was reminded of his aloneness, his potential mortality, and his own inability to create (2:16–18, 20b–22). Nonetheless, in his state of untried holiness, he remained genuinely innocent (2:25).

"You Will Surely Die"

After Adam and Eve disobeyed God by eating the forbidden fruit, they lost their naivete, hid in their guilt, made excuses for their sin, and inherited a harsher life (3:7–19). These realities were a psychospiritual taste of an upcoming physical death. Similarly when people cannot participate in life's most meaningful activities, they can experience an existential quality of deadness (Pss. 31:12; 88:1–18; Isa. 59:10).

Perhaps the most dramatic motif in the serpentine seduction is the denial-then-affirmation of the words:

"You will surely die!" (Gen. 2:16–17; 3:4, 19). Although Adam lived to be 930 years old (5:5), God declared the death verdict at the moment of disobedience.

The tree of life, the source of perpetual existence, was withdrawn from Adam and Eve to enact the death sentence (3:22–24). This banishment from the tree of life prevented Adam from indefinitely extending his potentially mortal life.[3]

While some people see this banishment as an act of mercy to prevent Adam from being eternally confined in a state of sin, it is more likely a simple statement of punishment. After all Adam had been given permission to eat from any tree except for the tree of knowledge of good and evil (2:16–17). But because of sin, God chose to withdraw the privilege of indefinite life extension, a privilege he will one day restore (Rev. 2:7; 22:2–3a, 14). Thus God, the sovereign clockmaker, prohibited humans from winding up their biological clocks. So death became the absence of physical life, the end result of a process of nonreplenishment of that life, and the ultimate spiritual separation from the divine source of life. While Adam's sin was the temporal cause of death, God's justice was the logical cause of death. While a criminal is responsible for the crime, the court is responsible for the sentence.

Dying Process Controlled by God

Though most of Israel's neighbor cultures viewed death as random, out of control, and malign, the Old Testament clearly affirmed death as being under God's control (Pss. 48:14; 68:20). All of life, whether agricultural, animal, or human, now takes part in a divinely established pattern of birth-then-death (Josh. 23:14; 1 Kings 2:1–2). Such a birth-then-death cycle implies that man lives once and dies at his divinely appointed time (Eccles. 3:1–2). With God so precisely in control, it is no wonder that the chronically ill would pray to him for healing (Ps. 13:3). Furthermore realistic faith sees healing as solely God's prerogative (Isa. 38:1–5).

Although we are frequently shocked by death (at least by its timing and causes), God is never surprised. After all, life and death are his business. Thus Hannah could prayerfully accept God's role in determining who would live and die, who would near death and who would rebound from that brink (1 Sam. 2:6). Because we are ignorant of how and when we will die, God's knowledge of these affairs stands in stark contrast to our vagueness (Gen. 27:2; Deut. 31:14).

If the Lord is sovereign over life and death, he can challenge his people to follow a certain course of action. Obedience to this course will result in an intensification of life, probably by quality and by quantity, while disobedience will result in a diminishment of life (Deut. 30:15–20).

While this truth obviously operates on a national level with Israel, it also operates on an individual level. People can die prematurely (earlier than they might have otherwise) by foolishly disobeying the Lord (Prov. 10:21; 11:19). While the fool chooses his or her course of action, it is God who chooses the divinely appropriate consequence of their action. Fortunately the corollary is also true for those who follow the Lord. For example Abraham died "full of years" (Gen. 25:8).

It is almost as though the biological alarm clock ticking away in each of us can be kept in a safe place to run its full course—or it can cast itself off of the dresser onto the floor. While the individual makes choices as to whether he or she will obey God and to what degree, God determines the basic destructibility of the clock that sends itself crashing to the floor. In his patience and mercy, of course, God can protect a fragile clock beyond its innate capabilities. After all, he is "not wanting anyone to perish" (2 Peter 3:9).

In summary then, Adam's swamp had three distinct realities. First, God created the human being as a physical/psychospiritual whole. Second, God instituted death as a divine judgment on sin. And third, God controls the living/dying process now. Having seen the basic realities, the critical question becomes how to survive, how the saints in the Old Testament era would cope with aging, grief, and death.

God's People Coped with Mortality

When the curse of death was lowered onto the earth, it blanketed every living thing—plant, animal, and human. Now from underneath that blanket of sad realities, the earth sings in a minor key. While God's people await a major key change, they have learned to sing in harmony with the earth. Through their own creativity and through divine guidance, Old Testament believers coped with their mortality rationally, ritually, and religiously. Through rational analysis they began to weigh individual deaths as relatively good or relatively bad. Through ritual customs they developed ways to express grief and honor toward lost loved ones. And through religious hope they grew to trust God's promises for the future.

Death: Good or Bad

Death is an intense and personal transition. Because it is, even fallen man, who is in the image of God, searches for a wider frame of meaning within which to interpret a death. Humans, unlike animals, can contemplate their own death and even take their own lives. Frequently humans use their higher analytical powers to pigeonhole a death as good or bad. Although death will always be a divine judgment on original sin, different scenarios allow us to tip the scales toward interpreting a particular death as relatively good or relatively bad. Though humans will never arrive at a consensus as to what makes a death good or bad, some biblical themes do emerge. And even if God's noblest creature cannot control whether, when, or how death will come, at least humans can seek an understanding of why a death comes, what meaning to attach to a death.

A good death. Through rational analysis, a particular death can be viewed positively when any of the following variables are prominent.

A Good Death Is When . . .

Death comes as a completion of maturity.	Job 5:26
Death follows a long, full life.	Gen. 25:8a
Death follows the rich blessings of God.	Num 23:10
Death follows the fulfillment of a hope.	Gen. 46:30
Death highlights a good reputation or posterity.	Isa. 56:5
Death comes at a time of interpersonal peace.	Jer. 34:4–5a
Death reveals the honest affection of friends.	Jer. 34:5b
Death reunites kin.	Gen. 25:8b
Death crystallizes one's hope in God.	Ps. 16:9–11
Death motivates a person toward wisdom.	Ps. 90:10, 12
Death rescues a sufferer from misery.	Job 3:20–22
Death purges a wicked person from society.	Gen. 6:7–8

A bad death. Similarly, death is often interpreted in a negative light when any of the following conditions prevail.

A Bad Death Is When . . .

Death seems premature.	Isa. 38:10
Death takes a child.	Lam. 2:11–12
Death is sudden or violent.	Ezek. 28:8
Death is by suicide.	1 Kings 16:18–19
Death comes through civil punishment on evil.	Exod. 22:18–19
Death comes as divine punishment on evil.	Nah. 1:14
Death leaves no heir.	Ruth 4:10

Customs for Grieving

In Old Testament society, when a loved one died the survivor had two responsibilities: to grieve in a healthy way and to treat the beloved's corpse with honor.

Good grief. With the death of a loved one, the closest family members and friends went into a period of mourning. On news of the death, a period of fasting would begin that might last as long as seven days (Gen. 50:10; 1 Sam. 31:13; 2 Sam. 12:16–18). Furthermore during the mourning period, those grieving would dress down so as not to appear celebrative. For instance, one might refrain from using perfumes or soaps (2 Sam. 12:20; 14:2). One could also tear clothing or wear sackcloth (Gen. 37:34; 2 Sam. 3:31; 13:31; 2 Kings 6:30; Job 1:20). If one were wearing headdress, it would likely be removed (Ezek. 24:17, 23). Such dress would capture the atmosphere of humility and sadness.

Generally grieving families would remain at home and receive visitors at the house. Thus those in mourning would remove their shoes and wait (Ezek. 24:17, 23). Sometimes the mourners would partially veil their faces as well (2 Sam. 19:4). Those visiting would often bring food to the nearest of kin since the uncleanness of the corpse prevented any food from being prepared in the house (Hos. 9:4).

When the visitors arrived, they might be greeted by the sight of mourners with their heads bowed in their hands or with their hands on their heads (2 Sam. 13:19; Jer. 2:37). Furthermore the visitors might encounter grieving persons placing dirt on themselves or sitting in the ash heap (Job 2:12). Such a custom, while far from western norms, was the Israelites' way of dramatizing the dust-to-dust principle of Genesis 3:19.

Sad poems and lament songs generally described the personal qualities of the deceased or the magnitude of the survivor's loss. These eulogizing laments could be offered by family (Gen. 50:10), friends (1 Sam. 25:1), prophets (2 Chron. 35:25), or poets (2 Sam. 1:17–27). This kind of ritualized reminiscence often continued right to the graveside (2 Sam. 3:31–34).

Bad grief. Old Testament believers grieved candidly and without embarrassment. Their only restraint involved avoiding occult practices like communicating with or feeding the dead (Deut. 18:10–11; 26:14) or like cutting one's body (Lev. 19:27–28; Deut. 14:1).

Handling the body. Not only did the bereaved try to care for themselves in a proper way, they were also concerned about giving due honor to the loved one's remains. Generally, the family would dress the deceased and carry the body on a bier (2 Sam. 3:31) to be buried on the day of death (Deut. 21:22–23). During this rite families showed public affection to the corpse (Gen.

50:1), even though this contact would temporarily render them ceremonially unclean (Num. 19:11–16).

The loved one's body was usually wrapped in a blanket and placed in a cave or tomb outside of city limits in a family-owned site (Gen. 23:19–20). In some cases incense and commemorative pillars might be used (2 Sam. 18:18; 2 Chron. 16:14), taking every precaution to protect the deceased's skeleton. On rare occasions Israelites were cremated (1 Sam. 31:12) or embalmed for delayed burial (Gen. 50:2–3, 26).

God's People Trusted His Promises

Though it is difficult to imagine living during the Old Testament era, the word pictures about death dating from that time do show some faint light of future hope. Numerous similes and metaphors such as the following about death are given by Old Testament writers, painting their picture of historic understanding.

Death Is Like . . .

Spilled water (2 Sam. 14:14)	Life is irretrievable.
A reaped harvest (Jer. 9:22)	Life is impossible to rejuvenate.
Exhaling (Job 14:10)	Life cannot be recaptured or seen.
Sleep (Ps. 13:3)	Life is not actively available.
Collapsing a tent (Isa. 38:12)	Life is out of sight.
Drowning (2 Sam. 22:5)	Life is out of sight.
Precious treasure (Ps. 116:15)	Life is of great value.

These images of death are a sobering picture of finality. Although death compels us into an invisible realm, God cares for us like a precious treasure, graciously attending to the needs of the dying person as well as for the departed saint.

Sheol: The Place of the Dead

Since grieving family members and friends usually said farewell to their loved one at the burial site, it is no wonder that descriptions of the grave and the afterworld were sometimes blended together. In fact, the Hebrew word *sheol* describes the place of the dead both literally and figuratively.

Descriptions of Sheol

A place of darkness	Job 10:21–22
of silence	Ps. 115:17b
of forgetfulness	Ps. 88:12
of ignorance	Job 14:21
of snares	2 Sam. 22:6
of no praise to God	Ps. 115:17a
where God forgets people	Ps. 88:5
of no hope in God	Isa. 38:18
with numerous inhabitants	Ezek. 32:18
of appointment	Job 30:23
like a large pit	Job 33:18
like a city with gates	Job 38:17
of weakness	Isa. 14:9–10
where all types of people go	Job 3:17–19
of reunion with kin	2 Sam. 12:23

After surveying such a morbid list of *sheol's* descriptions, the contemporary believer is advised to keep several observations in mind. First of all many of these descriptions are simple extensions of the grave, a place of darkness or silence, for instance. From the language of appearance these are accurate portraits of the realm of the dead.

Second, many of these pictures echo the sentiments of the bereaved survivors toward the grave, a place where the deceased remains uninformed about life's ongoing events, for example. These portrayals were true to the grieving family's reaction to the grave.

Third, these vignettes about *sheol* often capture the cessation element of death seen in the burial site, a place where one cannot praise the Lord or hope in God. For those in *sheol*, there is no more worship in the temple or hope that God will answer prayers for rescue from death. Needless to say the cessation theme is absolutely accurate in the realm of physical death.

Fourth, because death sometimes comes unexpectedly to us, it can be considered a snare, a trap to be avoided if possible.

Fifth, life experience teaches us that death is universal, with the grave housing all types of people.

But sixth, and finally, we have a basis for hope in looking forward to a reunion with beloved kin, since no one is annihilated in death. Although there is no clear compartmentalization between heaven and hell in these texts, we can expect to consciously and positively interact with those in the realm of the dead some day, presumably including fellowship with God himself.

Hope in the Face of Death

The God of hope seeks to fill us so that we overflow with hope (Rom. 15:13). And if hope is therefore so characteristic of God and of God's ministry to us, we would expect to find some reasons for hoping in the face of death, even during the Old Testament period. As noted already, the preciousness of our deaths may suggest an ongoing gracious concern of God, not just for the dying person but also for the departed saint. In addition the lack of personal annihilation suggests conscious, positive interaction in reunion with kin and in fellowship with God. Furthermore the Old Testament offers hope in the face of despair by showing that the curse pronounced on the serpent and on the earth (Gen. 3:13–19) is not placed directly on humans. Thus, God has left open the door for reunion, reconciliation, and fellowship with him.

We are also encouraged by the clear Old Testament hope for a future day of universal judgment (Job 19:25–27a; Prov. 14:32; Ezek. 39:21–22; Zeph. 3:8; Zech. 14:1–21). While the hope in these passages is focused on national judgment or on the vindication of an individual sufferer, there is clearly an underlying assumption of future justice. While most Old Testament believers had forsaken the idea of a just world where good things always happen to good people and bad things to bad people, they nonetheless believed in a just God. They fully expected him to validate truth and vindicate righteous behavior while retributing evil. These believers could only hope in God that any justice which had not yet been served at the time of death would be served at some divinely appointed future time. In this future day of judgment, Old Testament saints expected that God would separate between people whom he approved and disapproved (Dan. 12:2–3; Eccles. 12:13–14). Though no person is without sin, God will recognize those whom he has redeemed through the eternal effectiveness of Christ's redemption.

Not only did Old Testament saints hope for a future universal judgment between the righteous and the unrighteous, they also hoped for the end of death itself (Isa. 25:8; 26:19; 65:17–19, 25). Just as a wise king might work toward reconciling a wayward subject expelled from the court, so God will not allow death to be a per-

manent barrier to fellowship (2 Sam. 14:14). In fact in
God's ultimate victory, he will destroy death itself,
promising a resurrection which will dry the great river
of tears flowing from mankind.

Conclusion

Val's swamp, filled with deadly bacteria and a vicious
crocodile, would frighten anyone. Adam's Eden, shifting
instantly from a paradisical innocence to a poisoned
guilt, saddens even those who've never heard the earth
sing in her major key. But while the whole earth groans
in her minor key, awaiting the end of death's blanket-
ing curse, we can have hope (Rom. 8:25). We can hope
because God, the great musician, teaches us to groan
in harmony with the earth, while awaiting his major
transposition (Rom. 8:23). Even while we wait, the Holy
Spirit within us sings with melancholy harmony toward
that final day (Rom. 8:26). And until that final day, our
music will carry his lyrics of coming glory, freedom,
and redemptive purpose (Rom. 8:18–39).

Every song in a minor key, by lowering the third and
sixth tones of its scale, creates its eerie language. Likewise the early revelation of the Old Testament, by its
lowered tones, follows three rules for its pensive melody.
First, God created the human being as a physical/
psychospiritual whole. Second, God instituted death as
a divine judgment on sin. And finally, God controls the
living/dying process now.

Since we cannot choose to forcibly transpose the
earth's music, we must either learn to sing in minor harmony or we will sing in chaotic dissonance. Guided by
their musical instincts and the master musician, the
believers before Christ responded to aging, grief, and
death by singing three forms of empathic harmony. First,
God's people interpreted some deaths as good and others

as bad. Second, God's people developed customs for grieving and honorably disposing of loved ones' remains. And third, God's people grew to trust in the promises of God for the future. Fortunately God has promised to put the universe back into major harmony one day and to allow us again to eat from the Tree of Life (Rev. 21:1–5; 22:1–20).

Discussion Questions

1. How do you react to the simple holism of the early Old Testament?
2. When you consider the idea that man's breath is directly dependent on God, what implications does it hold for modern medical theory and the use of respirators?
3. How do you react to the theory that language of appearance explains the absence of explicit after-life references in some Old Testament passages?
4. Do you believe Adam had eaten from the Tree of Life before he was banished from Eden? Was his banishment an act of mercy or an act of judgment? What is the role of the tree in the new heavens and earth?
5. Do you believe that God controls the universal living/dying process, including how and when each individual dies? How does this concept fit with murder, suicide, artificial life support, abortion, and genetic engineering?
6. Which of the good death/bad death criteria appeal to you? Is it possible for one death to be viewed differently by two different people?
7. Which of the grief customs seem most familiar to you? Which ones would you be most likely to add to your grief repertoire? Which ones would be most difficult for you to practice? Why do you

think God forbade some grief customs? What do you think about praying to saints or conducting seances?

8. When you review the ways that corpses were treated in the Old Testament period, which ways seem appealing and which unappealing to you? How do you feel about same-day burials, cremation, embalming, coffins, and touching the deceased?

9. Which similes and metaphors about death seem most fitting to you, and why? Least fitting, and why?

10. How much hope did the Old Testament believers have in life beyond the grave? To what degree did they understand conscious, personal interaction in the afterworld and about heaven and hell?

3

How the New Testament Helps Us Face Aging, Grief, and Death

A ny New Testament study about aging, grief, and death ought to begin with the One who holds the keys to death (Rev. 1:18). Jesus Christ, in some of his most famous miracles and stories, summarizes his salient ideas about life, death, and afterlife. Although Lazarus of Bethany and Lazarus the beggar are probably not the same person, the inspired accounts bearing their name open a window into Jesus' theology of human destiny (Luke 16:19–31; John 11:1–12:19).

The Two Lazaruses

Lazarus of Bethany may well have suffered the death of his parents when he was young, leaving him to be raised by his two older sisters, Martha and Mary. With Martha's take-charge style, she may have become the provider for the threesome, while Mary's tenderness made her the nurturer. It's even possible that Martha earned some of their much needed income by working as a household servant in a wealthier neighbor's home. Just outside a household compound, such as the one where Martha might have worked, lay another Lazarus, the beggar. Apparently suffering from a chronic disease like leprosy, he was left to beg from passersby.

In time Jesus befriended Lazarus and his sisters in Bethany. He demonstrated the same kind of compassion toward them that he felt toward outcast beggars—beggars who craved the leftovers of those more fortunate than they—beggars whose constant companions were scavenging dogs.

Jesus, no doubt, challenged his friends from Bethany to anchor their faith in God, not in their medical or economic circumstances. In fact he went quite beyond traditional religious rhetoric: He challenged them to believe in him so that they would never die. Although Jesus may have been emphasizing the undying nature of their spiritual lives, he extended the sense to include an undying physical life as well. For those who would believe in him, there would never be a spiritual separation from God. Likewise for those who died believing in him, there would never be a permanent separation of their spirits from their bodies. And to prove the impermanence of their eventual physical deaths, Jesus proceeded to resurrect Lazarus of Bethany.

One can only imagine what it might have been like to be Lazarus of Bethany, resurrected. Days after dying, Lazarus must have awakened in his parents' tomb, wrapped in burial cloths. Jesus' words, "Lazarus, come out!" must have thundered in his ears. Conjecturing that Lazarus of Bethany was not permitted to recall or rehearse what he had experienced during those four days in the grave (2 Cor. 12:4), we can only imagine how Jesus might have described those days to Lazarus's curious friends: "The moment his heart stopped, I sent angels to pick him up in their arms like his mother used to do from his crib. They carried him instantly to paradise where he enjoyed an embrace from Abraham, his parents, and the other faithful there. He wasn't sick or harassed by life anymore."

Building on Jesus' story about the rich man and Lazarus (Luke 16:19–31), we might also venture to imagine how the Lord could have described the death of another, perhaps one like Martha's wealthy employer: "They really spent a royal fortune on his funeral in Jerusalem, resting his body near the royal tombs south of the city. But despite the fanfare, that man suffers in hell, not paradise, undergoing a fiery torture. Ever since he arrived in hell, he's been begging God to allow Lazarus to give him one drop of water. But God's answer has been a consistent, 'No! No one moves back and forth between paradise and hell after death!' Though this man had enjoyed the good life on earth, he has been begging God to send Lazarus back to warn his brothers so that they can avoid the sulfuric streets of the damned. But again, the answer has remained, 'No! Your brothers are alive and have the Scriptures to guide them. If they won't believe and obey God's Word, they certainly won't believe a man's word—even if that man had once been dead!'"

Theological Principles in the Lazarus Parables

From the accounts of Lazarus three theological principles arise concerning the nature of suffering, the rites of passage, and the truth about heaven and hell.

Suffering Is Universal

A simple reading of the Lazarus narratives captures the commonness of suffering: physical illness, social distress, emotional pain, bodily death, and potential torment. While God uniquely possesses immortality (1 Tim. 6:16), man dies and faces judgment (Heb. 9:27).

Hope in suffering. Despite the universal nature of suffering, Jesus identified Lazarus's death as purposeful: for the glory of God (John 11:4, 15). Though sufferers do not always know the reason for their troubles (John 9:1–3), Christ nonetheless emphasized a universal need to prepare for suffering and its consequences (Luke 13:1–5).

Also noteworthy is God's response (or lack of response) to the suffering. It is significant that much of the beggar's social distress persisted over a lifetime, and that Jesus didn't hurry to heal Lazarus's final illness (John 11:6). Instead the Lord was glad that his delay improved the spiritual opportunity for divine work (John 11:15). Similarly, the multiplied prayers of an afflicted apostle (2 Cor. 12:7–10) and of God's own Son in Gethsemane (Luke 22:39–46; Heb. 5:7–10) did not result in deliverance. If anything God granted them deliverance through (but not from) their trials. In a society that seeks to deny, avoid, escape, or deaden pain, it is surprising to realize that Christ refused any painkillers on the cross (Mark 15:23).

Love in suffering. Christ's most profound message to sufferers like Lazarus was sent by example. The Man of Sorrows authenticated the sufferer's lot by becoming a sufferer himself. In so doing he modeled the ministry that sufferers can have while they are in pain. In his example he didn't suggest that sufferers should be sickeningly pitied as if they were hopeless or in need of a panicky quick fix. To the contrary, Christ ministered even during his suffering:

Healing the temple soldier's ear (Luke 22:50–51)

Giving prophetic warning to the mourners on the Via Dolorosa (23:27–31)

Praying for forgiveness for his executioners (v. 34)

Reaching out to the thieves crucified on either side of him (vv. 39–43)

Arranging for Mary's and John's mutual adoption (vv. 26–27)

Rites of Passage Are Valuable

In Lazarus's culture, as in ours, rites of passage signal that a major change has taken place. These familiar customs affirm group beliefs, relationships, and roles in society.

The rites of passage. In first-century Israel, the bereaved family washed the dead body of their loved one, wrapped it in clean linen cloths (John 11:44; Matt. 27:59; Acts 5:6), pouring spices, perfumes, ointments, and flower petals in between the layers of burial wrappings (Luke 23:56; John 19:39–40). The unembalmed deceased was then carried on an open bier to a grave site (Luke 7:14; Acts 5:10), was interred on the same day, and began decomposing (John 11:17, 39).

The community message. The washing and wrapping of Lazarus's body signaled the dignity and loving respect due the divinely created body. The fragrances expressed grief over the dust-to-dust destiny of the loved one, seeking to dull the initial impact of decay for mourners. The open bier invited the community at large to recognize the deceased and to join the mourning processional. The same-day burial illustrated the realism of those grieving and their concern for household hygiene.

Unlike their pagan contemporaries, the early Christians knew that the treatment of the corpse did not affect the departed person (Matt. 10:28). Rather, death rites allowed the living to communicate richly with one another in the mutual healing process (John 11:36).

Jesus not only underwent this kind of burial himself (1 Cor. 15:4), he affirmed the importance of this transition by sending angels at death to protect the beggar Lazarus's body (Luke 16:22; Jude 9).

Heaven and Hell Are Real

It has become common in the twentieth century to deny, ignore, or redefine the doctrine of everlasting punishment. The life of Lazarus and the words of Christ, however, militate against this trend.

Christ, the supreme power over death. In the story of Lazarus Jesus shines as One who is unafraid of his own coming death (John 11:8–10) and around whom others can rally in the face of their deaths (John 11:16). Lazarus's story thus fitly climaxes with Christ's raising him from the dead (John 11:43–44). Though death is powerful, Christ is more powerful, and one day he will cast death and hell into the lake of fire (John 11:25–26; Rom. 6:9; 1 Cor. 15:22, 25–26, 54–57; Heb. 2:14–15; Rev. 20:14).

Two alternatives after death. If Christ reigns supreme over death, it is reasonable that he would know the fate of those that die (Luke 16:19–25). In his teaching, he describes one who lived a life of wealth and comfort only to inherit fiery torment after death. Fortunately he tells of another fate as Lazarus inherits the bliss of paradise following his beggarly life.

Some would suppose that Christ's opposite portraits of the rich man and the beggar in the afterworld were born out of the Lord's deep sense of social justice. They would imagine that Christ saw eternity as granting inverse retribution to these men, eternally balancing the scales against their fortunes in life. When one compares the whole of Christ's teaching, however, his story about the rich man and Lazarus merely echoes the ancient principle that man looks at the outward appearance but the Lord looks at the heart (1 Sam. 16:7). Furthermore a straightforward reading of Jesus' story yields four simple truths which were relevant to these men, rich or poor, as they are to all humankind.

Afterlife Is . . .

A conscious, interactive existence	Luke 16:23–31
A severe two-way destiny: heaven vs. hell	Luke 16:22–25
Without a second chance for repentance	Luke 16:26
Beyond the realm of communicating with the living	Luke 16:27–31

Faith in Christ is the sole criterion. Christ not only frames the mutually exclusive destinies of heaven and hell but he also pinpoints the single variable that determines which fate we inherit. In the Lazarus accounts and elsewhere, that sole criterion for heaven is variously described as: listening to the testimony of Scripture (Luke 16:29), hearing Christ's word (John 5:24), repenting (Luke 16:30), believing in Christ (John 11:25–27), believing in the Son (John 3:36), believing in the Father (John 5:24), keeping Christ's word (John 8:51), being a sheep on the right side of God (Matt. 25:33), blessed by the Father (Matt. 25:34), and being one of the righteous (Matt. 13:43). Those who have this saving faith in Christ are destined to experience the realities of heaven.

The Heavenly Inheritance of the Saints

Having eternal life	Matt. 25:46
Having no condemnation	John 5:24
Passing from death to life	1 John 3:14
Being comforted at Abraham's side	Luke 16:22–25
Being with Jesus in Father's house	John 14:2–3
Being relieved from trouble	2 Thess. 1:7
Rising again	John 11:23
Never dying	John 11:26
Entering the Kingdom of Heaven	Matt. 7:21
Shining like the sun	Matt. 13:43
Having all tears wiped away by God	Rev. 7:17

Conversely, those who do not possess the key to a heavenly destiny are described as: believing not the Son (John 3:36), not obeying the gospel of Christ (2 Thess. 1:8), remaining in death (1 John 3:14), being evildoers (Matt. 7:23), having left the straight way (2 Peter 2:15), being weeds to be burned (Matt. 13:40–42), and being goats on the left side of God (Matt. 25:33, 41). Thus, those who fail to meet Christ in faith are destined to inherit the hellish realities.

The Hellish Inheritance of the Unredeemed

Not seeing life/remaining under God's wrath	John 3:36
A forced departure from the presence of God	Matt. 7:23
Being in a tormenting and unending hellfire prepared for Satan and demons	Matt. 5:22, 29–30; 10:28; 25:41, 46

Never being forgiven	Matt. 12:32
Being thrown into a place of dark-ness, weeping, teeth gnashing, and burning	Matt. 8:12; 13:40–42; 22:13
Being punished with everlasting destruction	2 Thess. 1:9
Being put in gloomy dungeons	2 Peter 2:4, 17
Being bound with everlasting chains	Jude 6

No message is taught in the Scriptures more often or more earnestly than the necessity of faith in Christ—for good reason.

Theological Principles beyond the Lazarus Parables

Beyond the Lazarus narratives, the New Testament enlarges on three other questions related to the living/dying pattern: *How did it start? What is it like today? How will it end?*

The Beginning of the Living/Dying Pattern

According to the New Testament, the living/dying pattern began as a result of Adam's disobedience (Rom. 5:19; 1 Cor. 15:22). While people have always been tempted to presume that an individual's death is the exclusive result of the dead person's sin, the apostle Paul points instead to a domino effect begun in Eden. If our deaths were always and only the result of personal sin, Christ would never have died. In reality we all die—Christ included—because of the first Adam. However because of choices we or others make, the timing and means of our deaths may vary. Even in such cases, any timing and means that may seem off-time to us have always been incorporated into the plan of God.

The Present Status of the Living/Dying Pattern

According to various New Testament writers, the timeless essence of dying is captured by the following metaphors.

Sleep	1 Thess. 4:13	The body is at rest.
Absence	2 Cor. 5:8	The spirit separates from the body.
Departure	2 Tim. 4:6	The immaterial self travels to meet God.
Gain	Phil. 1:21	The deceased attains true advantage.

In addition to these metaphors the Bible clearly presents death as a humanly irreversible separation from the body and warns anyone who wants to learn about the afterworld to heed the Scriptures, not the perceptions of some astral traveler (Luke 16:30–31).

The Projected End of the Living/Dying Pattern

The living/dying pattern, begun in Eden and touching us today, will end when Jesus returns to vanquish death (Rev. 19:11, 16; 20:10, 14; 21:3–4). Thus, the living/dying pattern will end after two future resurrections are completed. These resurrections are given numerous labels in the New Testament.

The Resurrection of Believers

The first resurrection	Rev. 20:5–6
The resurrection of the righteous	Luke 14:14
The resurrection to life	John 5:28–29

The better resurrection	Heb. 11:35
The resurrection from the dead	Phil. 3:10–11
The narrow road that leads to life	Matt. 7:14

The Resurrection of Unbelievers

The resurrection to damnation	John 5:28–29
The second death	Rev. 20:6, 13–15
The broad road leading to destruction	Matt. 7:13

Some Christians (premillenialists) believe that the resurrection of believers is anchored in Christ's resurrection (1 Cor. 15:20–23a) and previewed by the rapture of the church (1 Cor. 15:23b; 1 Thess. 4:13–17).[1] It takes place just prior to the thousand-year kingdom (1 Cor. 15:24–26), bringing Old Testament and tribulation saints back to life (Isa. 26:19; Rev. 20:1–6). In contrast, the resurrection of unbelievers follows the millennium and leads to everlasting punishment (Dan. 12:2; Rev. 20:11–15).

Epilogue on Gehenna

With predictive realism, an angry prophet stood just south of Jerusalem in Wadi Errababi. Jeremiah, incensed on behalf of God, prophesied judgment against those sacrificing their children to Moloch in the valley (Jer. 7:32; 19:6). The ugly picture of their smoldering corpses, foul smell, and dark beliefs became the earthly image of an eternal judgment yet to come (Isa. 31:9; 66:24).[2] But mercifully, whether in the days of Jeremiah or Lazarus, the One who wants none to perish has offered a redemptive, heavenly rest to our souls (2 Peter 3:9; Matt. 11:28–29).

Discussion Questions

1. Meditate on Jesus' statements about himself in John 11:25 and Revelation 1:17–18. Brainstorm all the possible implications of these words, ranking them from the most meaningful to least meaningful for you.

2. Can you think of any miracles or discourses of Jesus, other than those with Lazarus, that help summarize the Lord's teachings on aging, grief, and death? List the central ideas from at least one incident or text.

3. What principles about suffering found in the New Testament are most likely to help you? Name one area where you need to improve most as a caregiver.

4. Name at least three rites of passage used in Lazarus's day and three in ours. What purpose does each rite serve?

5. What descriptions of heaven and hell are most moving to you? Why do you think the Bible spends more time arguing for the importance of faith in Christ than describing the differences between heaven and hell? What are the implications of this priority for ministry?

6. If you were to put the following topics into your own words, how would you describe the nature of heaven; the nature of hell; how one becomes destined for heaven; how one becomes destined for hell?

7. Which metaphor of death is most helpful to you? Which might be most helpful to children? To sufferers?

8. What correlations do you see between out-of-body and near-death experiences and the New Testament?

9. Draw a time line of the future based on Jesus' return to earth and the future resurrections.
10. Brainstorm comparisons between the Hinnom Valley and Gehenna.

Part 2

Personal Caregiving

Introduction

In 1896, when Fort Randall Cemetery was being moved to a new location, the exhumations provided some startling discoveries. One soldier, struck by lightning, had apparently revived shortly after burial, pushing open his casket lid. Other corpses were found clutching their clothes tightfistedly. A thirty-five-year-old man, supposedly dead of scarlet fever, had shattered the glass front of his coffin, kicked out the bottom, and sprung the sides. The unfortunate deceased lay face down, arms bent, holding handfuls of his own hair.[1]

Many individuals fear death; for some, it is the fear of being buried alive. Before the era of widespread embalming, when estimates suggest that as many as 2 percent of those interred were buried alive, such a fear was based on a well-founded possibility.

In Part 2, we will learn how the individual experiences aging, grief, and death from a psychosocial perspective. As individuals we sometimes see the sun rising on the horizon like the ever-nearing and sometimes-fearful knowledge of certain death. As individuals we sometimes watch the sun pass overhead and set on the far horizon like the farewells of grief. Some of us will respond creatively to the challenges of aging, to living realistically between the horizons. Others, to avoid the pain, may hurl themselves at the horizon, taking destiny into their own hands. By God's grace, we will travel compassionately, helping fellow pilgrims, young and old, as they face their sundown and coming dawn.

4

The Fear of Death

Dorothy? . . . Steve's been shot!" The chilling words rifled through the phone, staggering the suburban housewife as if she'd been shot. "A madman is loose in the AmeriBusiness Building, shooting everybody in sight!"

The "Tin Can" Trauma

The caller, only half-right, had begun to tell about the deranged gunman who was launching a one-man assault on the "Tin Can," the AmeriBusiness Building where Steve was Chief Engineer. Dozens of employees, dead and wounded, littered hallways and offices as co-workers frantically poured out of every exit. One man in a pool of blood had been mistaken as Steve, setting off the call from the police perimeter. But Steve was still alive, trapped inside his high-tech war zone, fighting for his life against a Vietnam vet disgruntled over his job.

The terrorist had throttled his luxury car into the lobby to begin his rampage. Stepping out of his steaming car in battle fatigues, his Israeli submachine gun tore the lobby guard nearly in half. Sporting an arsenal of weapons and ammunition, this Rambo began stalking unarmed and anonymous employees. Anyone stepping into the hallway to decipher the chaos was picked off like a duck in a shooting gallery.

Because individual offices could not be locked, frightened men and women went scrambling under desks as valiant office mates held doors shut, praying that no blast would penetrate their trembling backs.

Steve, needing to determine where his opponent was, listened like a hunter. Hearing the deadly "click" of a slide action shotgun, Steve yanked his head back into the room, sensing that the killer was just around the corner. Moments later, a fatal blast ended the life of another staffer venturing out of a further doorway.

In time Steve would be able to escape the psychotic terror of those familiar halls. But no sooner would he find himself safely outside than the police would recruit him to lead them back in so they could stalk their mass murderer, rescuing the wounded and hidden. Positioned behind a metal shield, Steve would guide the SWAT team through the passageways that he knew like the back of his hand.

Long hours after the maniac's declaration of war, the psychopath would be under arrest, and Dorothy would learn that Steve was safe. Though not wounded in body, Steve would painfully relive those hours again and again. "Afraid to die? I guess like anyone else. But I was ready to die," he'd repeat. "What about my work partner? Alive one minute, murdered the next. Had he ever heard the gospel from my lips? Am I living like today could be my last?"

These and a thousand other questions have troubled the heart of those made tender by death with questions like: How should we feel toward our own death and toward the death of others? Is it possible to be too fearful of death or not fearful enough? Does Christ take away our fear of death? In this chapter we seek to answer three heartfelt questions: *What does it mean to be afraid of death? Who is afraid of death?* And *how does our attitude toward death affect our behavior?*

What Is Death Anxiety?

Death anxiety is "an unpleasant emotional state precipitated by contemplating one's own death."[1] Though theories on the origin of the fear of death vary widely, there is general agreement on the four elements which characterize it.[2]

Anticipatory Socialization: Thinking ahead about our death

Concerns about the Dying Process: Imagining the changes associated with our final illness, injury, or postmortem decay

Awareness of Time: Sensing the amount and rapidity of time between today and our death

Pain: Measuring the stresses expected with our dying

To clarify these four elements, a simple illustration of each can serve the point.

Anticipatory Socialization

Larry's love for sports finally convinced his dad to put a concrete basketball court in the backyard. "Can't you stay home from work today, Dad, and play one-on-one with me?" the twelve-year-old pleaded. With the pole and backboard in place, it seemed only right to inaugurate the court together. After a quick call to the office, the father-and-son duo were ready to celebrate the new court and the joy of being together.

But tragically, during that morning of loving laughter and hard-earned sweat, Larry's dad dropped dead of a massive heart attack. Paralyzed by false guilt, Larry would blame himself for years. Obsessed with the idea that he had killed his father, he pondered who he might kill next given the extreme frailty of life.

Larry was struggling with magical thought, the childish idea that he was responsible for something beyond his control. Until Larry received help, he often thought ahead to his own death and the death of others. Convinced that death lurked just around an arbitrary corner, this grieving boy needed to expand his awareness of his father's multiple causes of death: an undiagnosed heart condition, the lack of physical fitness, his father's choice to stay home and play harder than he was capable of playing, and so forth.

When it comes to the fear of death, our specific thoughts and feelings contribute to the overall nature and intensity of our anxiety. For Larry, his anticipatory socialization was dramatically affected by his shocking experience in the backyard that day.

Concerns about the Dying Process

"You didn't have anything to do today, did you?" the father drilled his son, interrogation style. Hesitating to lie, the boy mouthed, "Well . . ." Glaring, the father shot back, "Couldn't have been as important as this!" backing the old sedan into the street.

Passing the first few miles in silence, the boy steeled himself against tears, puzzled by the behavior of his usually reclusive father. "Where are we going?" he explored meekly. "To the city . . . to the cemetery," the driver retorted in telegraph-style staccato. Again silence swallowed up conversation.

Within the hour, two silhouettes stood, untouching, at the unmarked grave of the elder's mother. Though an unspoken heritage for the boy, the story of his paternal grandmother would be once whispered beside the browning shrubbery, opening a window into his father's past. Staring at the little number tab in the unmown grass at Cedar Hill, words became pictures: "Dad was weak and absent, a baker for a while, till he disappeared into the bottle. Mom was sick with heart disease, seven kids, poor as dirt. I helped her raise my brothers and sisters till she died and I went away to war."

The pause seemed like an eternity. "Do you know why I work every day, putting food on the table and a roof overhead?" the melancholy man queried with a blank stare. "So you will take care of me when I'm old; so I won't die alone, hungry, and poor."[3] This man, on that Saturday, was reaching back and peering ahead. Afraid to die? Probably not. Concerned about dying a certain way? Yes.

Awareness of Time

A woman, awaiting results on a series of diagnostic tests, was confidently informed by her physician, "We're pretty sure it's cancer." Trusting the doctor's expertise, this woman began to grieve in light of her prognosis. Fortunately for the woman, the test results came back several days later showing no trace of cancer. With good cause, this relieved patient began seriously questioning the physician's medical and ethical judgment, having been driven into an anxious panic by him, temporarily adopting a much more compressed sense of the time she had left to live.

Measuring the Physical Pain
Involved in the Dying Process

Often, when people are confronted with death, their fear focuses on the pain they expect to endure. On the day Pearl Harbor was bombed, a chaplain addressed anxious midshipmen at the U.S. Naval Academy, telling of a mother whose child was also facing imminent death. Hoping she would never have to tell the sad news to her son, the mother was caught off guard while reading to him about King Arthur. Pondering the fate of so many fair knights, the pensive child looked into his mother's eyes, asking, "What is it like to die? Does it hurt?" With tears streaming down her cheeks, she breathed a prayer for wisdom and reminded her boy of those days when he had played so hard that he would fall asleep on the floor, still dressed. The little lad, clearly remembering the joy of waking up in his own bed the morning after those weary days, was reassured that his loving father had carried him in strong arms into his own room. Understanding the parallel to his coming death, he took comfort that he could fall asleep in the arms of Jesus, ready to awake at dawn in his Father's house.[4]

Although each person exhibits a unique composition of the fear of death, the characteristic building blocks are often present and timelessly biblical: thinking ahead about death (Ps. 90:12), imagining the dying process (Gen. 49:28–50:1), sensing how much time is left (James 4:14–15), and measuring expectant pain (Matt. 10:28).

Who Is Afraid of Death?

Not only is it valuable to describe what it means to be afraid of death, it is also useful for people helpers to be able to identify which people are characteristically high or low in death anxiety. According to research[5] death anxiety is generally not correlated to our age, physical health, occupation, or our social interests. However, there are other specific correlates to high and low levels of death anxiety.

Levels of Death Anxiety

Based on empirical investigation,[6] we can identify six qualities of life which are generally correlated with those who have characteristically higher levels of death anxiety.

What kinds of people often have high death anxiety?

1. Spiritually insecure people who:
   Are less personally devout
   Are less certain about religion in general
   Don't believe in afterlife
   Don't attend church regularly
   Are Jews
   Are Catholics
   Are psychiatric patients who left the religion of
      their youth
   Are anxious about the passage of time
   Perceive time lived as much greater than time left
   Have low self-actualization
   Have low purpose in life
   Have low life-satisfaction
   Have low death-acceptance
   Have low feelings of energy and competence for
      difficult tasks
   Have low death transcendence: facing death
      regretfully
   Have low meditative awareness: not calm and
      inner-centered
   Have high need to achieve and who aren't highly
      religious
   Are dogmatic
   Are teetotalers

2. Emotionally vulnerable people who:
   Are females
   Are firstborns
   Are depressed retired persons
   Have a negative self-image
   Have lesser psychological endurance
   Have less ego strength
   Are inclined toward hypochondriasis
   Are sensitizers in the Myers-Briggs Temperament typology
   Are stress-sensitive first-year medical students
   Are nurturant females majoring in social work or education
   Are introverted college students likely to admit weaknesses
   Visit the elderly but not their own grandparents
   Are psychiatric patients
   Are grieving a death within the previous two years
   Are victims of rape

3. Chronically high stressed people who:
   Are firefighters
   Are policemen
   Are ICU personnel
   Are nursing students in their first two years
   Are younger and less-experienced physicians
   Are penitentiary inmates
   Are patients on kidney dialysis
   Are older adults with insomnia
   Are elderly women with health problems
   Are hospice volunteers who quit within the first year

4. Close family members of a death-anxious person:
   Married person whose spouse is death-anxious
   Child whose parent of the same sex is death-anxious
   Children with a death-anxious sibling
   College students with a death-anxious grandmother
   Wives of patients on kidney dialysis

5. People whose support system is weaker:
   Blacks
   Homosexuals
   Urban dwellers
   Never married
   High school students who live with only one parent
   Those with poverty level or lower income level

6. People with few coping skills:
   With less social/interpersonal adequacy
   With an external locus of control
   With lower educational and IQ levels
   People who smoke a few cigarettes per day
   People attempting a suicide with high rescue potential
   College students who believe suicide is a right
   Delta alcoholics: maintenance drinkers who don't binge

Although one can infer some potential associations with low-death anxiety by reversing the previous findings, the literature review previously cited goes on to suggest five generalized correlations with lower levels of death anxiety.

What kinds of people often have lower death anxiety?

1. Spiritually self-assured persons:
   Strongly religious
   Protestants
   Born again
   Hospice volunteers with purpose in life
   Feel they've been given more time after a near
     death experience
   Strongly nonreligious

2. Emotionally invulnerable persons:
   Repress their feelings
   Military officers
   Pragmatic males majoring in business
   With a strong sense of well-being
   With ego strength

3. Persons who have learned to live with chronic stress:
   Older adults
   Terminal cancer patients
   Huntington's chorea patients
   Nurses with at least five years' experience
   Hospice volunteers with at least one year of
     experience

4. Persons with a strong support systems:
   Nursing home residents who perceive their care
     as good
   Elderly men in domiciliary care who view them-
     selves as well

5. Persons with numerous coping skills:
>   People who show concern for themselves
>   Elderly patients with a positive attitude toward
>   euthanasia
>   Interpersonal trust
>   Inclined toward extraversion

It would seem from research correlates that two factors largely influence the nature and intensity of death anxiety: one's psychospiritual wellness and one's life experiences. It therefore becomes imperative that the skillful caregiver seek to develop a model for facilitating relevant changes in attitude and lifestyle.

How Death Anxiety Affects Behavior

Chart 1 illustrates how our ratio of death anxiety to self-reliance determines our particular lifestyle.

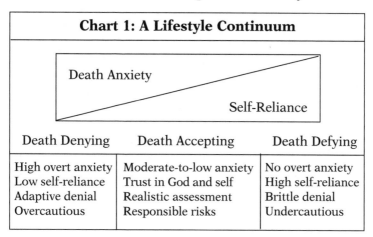

Chart 1: A Lifestyle Continuum		
Death Denying	Death Accepting	Death Defying
High overt anxiety	Moderate-to-low anxiety	No overt anxiety
Low self-reliance	Trust in God and self	High self-reliance
Adaptive denial	Realistic assessment	Brittle denial
Overcautious	Responsible risks	Undercautious

In this model a person's overt death anxiety blends with his or her overt sense of competence for meeting the challenges of life and death. One's particular blend of death anxiety and personal mastery results in a continuum on which three respective lifestyles can be plotted.

The Death-Denying Lifestyle

A person toward the left end of this continuum is highly death-anxious and struggles to keep feelings of helplessness and dread under control. To minimize such discomfort, this person tries to avoid any situation that would risk premature death or be reminiscent of coming mortality. Because this person feels unable to cope with the threat of death, there may be a tendency to withdraw from settings perceived to be dangerous. It would also be common for such a person to simply change the subject whenever a conversation became too realistic.

The story of one Vietnam veteran illustrates the behavioral struggle of this death-denying lifestyle. After seeing his best friends killed before his eyes from an enemy mortar attack, one G.I. began to experience a kind of behavioral paralysis born of high anxiety and low self-reliance. Back in the USA, he engaged in efforts to protect himself from the haunting feeling that it could happen again. He coped with his anxiety by refusing to drive over 35 miles per hour, by refusing to leave his house at night, and by refusing to allow his wife and children to be away from home simultaneously.

The apostle Peter pinpointed the inherent dangers in this lifestyle. According to the inspired fisherman, people with such a lifestyle feel they can't grapple with the obvious future and thus try to live in an eternal present (2 Peter 3:4). For them, the narcotic of immediate comfort often helps dull the pain of their inevitable demise (2 Peter 1:4; 2:1–22). But rather than adopting the death-denying lifestyle, Peter exhorts believers to develop a holy lifestyle, deferring their ultimate gratification until the return of Christ (1 Peter 1:6–7; 2 Peter 3:12).

The Death-Defying Lifestyle

Toward the right end of the continuum, a person may be unaware of any conscious anxiety toward death. Instead, this person could have an exaggerated sense of immortality, feeling absolutely in control of destiny and playing Russian roulette with life. Far from avoiding risk and danger, this person may flirt with the more morbid aspects of life, enjoying the hysterical attention it generates but arrogantly reasoning, "It will never happen to me!" Such an attitude can sponsor risky behavior.

The story of another Vietnam vet illustrates the struggles of the death-defying lifestyle. Following the war Jimmy's civilian life became increasingly risky and para-suicidal. He took to flying ultralights, to using semi-automatic assault weapons, and to following impulsive instincts to batter people. Bouncing in and out of court for venting his destructive rage, his ultimate act made national headlines.[7] On May 9, 1989, Jimmy purchased 1,400 rounds of rifle ammunition, brutally murdered his ex-wife in her home, and hijacked a Cessna 152 from the local airport. Flying through Boston's night sky, this terrorist fired wildly at Red Sox fans leaving Fenway Park, at the Prudential Tower Skywalk, at parked cars, and at Logan's Air Traffic Control Towers. Eventually, because he was running low on fuel and was no longer inebriated with his distorted power, authorities were able to arrest this death defier.

But concerning such attitudes, the apostle James focuses scriptural scrutiny on the death-defying lifestyle. Burdened for poor and abused laborers, James confronted their bosses: arrogant merchants who behaved as though the future were subject merely to their own calculations (James 2:1–9; 4:13–17; 5:4–6). Instead of defying death, James challenged his readers to own up to their frailty and to patiently depend on the Lord (James 4:14; 5:7–8).

The Death-Accepting Lifestyle

Toward the midrange of the lifestyle continuum are people who truly know that death is coming. They don't naively look forward to death; there's much that they still love about life. Yet they've accepted their mortality and have purposed to live life realistically and intentionally. They allow death to motivate them to live wisely, balancing what they can do and what they must depend on God and others to do. They also strike a good balance of knowing when to take a worthwhile risk while avoiding both extremes of foolhardiness and over-protectiveness.

This healthy balance has been described in the Bible as the *pilgrim lifestyle* (1 Peter 2:11; Heb. 11:8–10). Paul, an example of this balance, fully considered himself a citizen of heaven; yet he made responsible choices on earth (Phil. 3:20–21). He made plans for the future, plans which were profitable according to the Word of God, while remaining personally flexible for God to redirect any of those well-made plans (Acts 13–14; 16:9–10). This apostle to the Gentiles set his goal to know Christ intimately and to make the most of living for him until death ended his day of opportunity (Phil. 1:21; 3:10).

Early believers who had this pilgrim balance did not flee or compromise in the face of death (Acts 6:8–7:60; 20:24), affirming that they did not live on the left end of the spectrum. Furthermore these noble witnesses refused to provoke hostile persecution arrogantly (Matt. 27:14; Acts 26; 1 Peter 3:15), suggesting that they didn't come from the right end of the model either. These believers learned the lesson of Jesus who took up his cross and was ready to die, if and when the will of God summoned. The Master taught his followers to accept their own mortality in advance and to prepare for the ultimate test of their faith ahead of time. His example and teaching led his disciples to commit themselves to those things which transcend physical death, orienting their daily behavior to the eternal values of the sojourner's life. They learned the lesson of Luther who wrote:

> Let goods and kindreds go,
> This mortal life also—
> The body they may kill,
> God's truth abideth still:
> His kingdom is forever.[8]

Jesus and the Fear of Death

Some people apparently have too much fear about death. They become Satan's paranoid prey as he holds them in bondage to rituals which they believe will protect them but which ultimately will destroy them (Heb. 2:14–15). On the other hand, those people who have too little concern about death often play satanic jeopardy with the precious commodity of life. When Adam and Eve were warned not to eat the forbidden fruit lest they die (Gen. 2:17), they minimized the predicted danger and were seduced out onto fatally thin ice. Similarly Satan tempted the Lord to plummet himself from the temple roof (Matt. 4:5–7).

In Jesus Christ we have the potential for being healed from pathological levels of death anxiety, both from having too much or too little real regard for man's final appointment (Heb. 9:27). In Christ, we can be freed from the fear of annihilation because the Bible teaches us that death does not end it all. We can be freed from the fear of the unknown because Christ speaks to us from beyond the grave. We can be freed from the fear of damnation because Jesus offers us an abundantly forgiven life. We can be freed from the fear of being alone because the Good Shepherd leads his sheep through the valley of the shadow of death. But despite these assurances, Christ nowhere diminishes our healthy interest in living a life that counts for eternity, a life spiritually rich with gold, silver, and costly stones rather than the tawdry life of wood, hay, and straw (1 Cor. 3:12). Indeed, it is only through a death-transcending love for Life himself that our obituary could ever read like the martyrs to come: "They did not love their lives so much as to shrink from death" (Rev. 12:11).

The "Tin Can" Revisited

Years after the frightening trauma at the Ameri-Business Building Steve was again surrounded by death. But this time death was not coming through demented rifle fire. Instead the terror of Lou Gehrig's disease was rapidly ruining the body and brain of Steve's dad, Jolly Henry.

Aptly caricatured by his nickname, Steve's dad had been the joyful picture of tireless work. While running his little grocery store, no customer could leave his premises without an evangelistic tract. "So what if they throw them in the trash?" he'd say, smiling. "The Lord must know there's a garbage man out there who needs the gospel!" The long years of running ice cream trucks in the community had outfitted one small church after another with pencils or pews, whatever was most pressing. Through the Gideons Jolly Henry had been responsible for delivering thousands of New Testaments and Bibles into the right hands.

But now the friendly workaholic was up against the challenge of his lifetime. Jolly Henry was on the last lap of a six-month marathon from diagnosis to death. This once intensely independent man now needed others to feed and toilet him. Unable to muster strength beyond lifting his fingers and wagging his head, Jolly had been moved to Winchester Hospital with end-stage pneumonia. His valiant wife, supported by adult children, had tried to keep him at home where he had wanted to be. But when Jolly fell like dead weight onto Mrs. Henry while being moved from the bed to the wheelchair, she lay pinned, leaving both of them crying until relief arrived.

Straining to speak at the hospital, Jolly felt as if his tongue had been wrapped with cotton. With exhausting effort and mere head nods, the time-weary warrior made several things clear: no ICU, no CPR, no chest tube, no ventilator, all by a man who knew he'd strangle to death! Jolly had one medical goal: get well enough to go home to die.

But those days in the hospital were not days of dreadful fear; they were days of laughter, tears, and memories. Visitors were treated like royalty as the gracious but dying host hoarsely entertained his guests. As friends would rehearse the goodness of the Lord over the years, he'd mouth, "Oh, my!" again and again. With the help of one of the children, Jolly placed a catalog order that would deliver anniversary presents to his wife, knowing that he wouldn't be there to celebrate when the time came.

After wrestling with the "Why?" of his dreaded disease, Jolly gave up needing to understand; he only needed grace to be faithful. It had been the same way when the Lord led him to move out of state to begin a ministry of grocery store evangelism and Gideon work. It hadn't all made sense at the time but now it did. He could even come to peace with his son's decision not to enter the U.S. Naval Academy. If Steve had prayed about it and the Lord had given him peace, then going to Washington Bible College and engaging in a bivocational church-and-engineering ministry was okay with Jolly.

With the pneumonia stabilized, Jolly was given his wish to return home. Amidst an army of paramedics and oxygen equipment, he knew it was time to begin saying goodbye. As the medical technicians explained the complexities of his oxygen equipment, Jolly turned toward his kids with a grin and a wink, signaling, "We're not going to need all that!"

As the strangers departed, the family members were called in one at a time. Like Jacob on his deathbed, Jolly offered words of final blessing and warning to each. Then, as if he were the master conductor of a family chorus, Jolly started his family singing the old favorites straight through the hymnbook. Between each selection, he'd mouth the words of a long-loved Scripture in his raspy whisper. The circle remained unbroken until the Gentle Shepherd took him all the way home.

Discussion Questions

1. Imagine yourself as the disgruntled employee on his shooting rampage. What are you thinking and feeling?
2. When did you come nearest to death? How did you respond at the time and later? How did other people respond at the time and later?
3. Rank the four elements of the fear of death from the one that gives you the greatest concern to the least concern: anticipatory socialization, concerns about the dying process, awareness of time, and pain.

4. Reflect on your own life experiences until you can give at least one example of magical thought, brittle denial, adaptive denial, overcautiousness, undercautiousness.

5. Imagine you were the young boy at the cemetery whose father asked for help with his concerns about dying in old age, alone, hungry, and poor. Have you ever had such a conversation with someone about his/her death?

6. Have you ever had your sense of time severely altered, either by gaining an expanded sense of time or an urgently compressed sense of time? What impact did it have on you?

7. Consider the six generalizations about people who are higher in death anxiety. Which generalizations seem obviously correct to you and which ones seem harder to explain? Analyze the five low-anxiety generalizations in the same way.

8. When you are not living the balanced lifestyle of the Christian pilgrim, toward which end of the continuum do you tend to drift? What do Jesus' words about taking up his cross mean for the person who is in spiritual balance?

9. How is it possible to have too much fear or too little fear about death? Where do those in Satan's bondage fit? Where would Adam and Eve have fit?

10. Imagine yourself as Jolly Henry dying of Lou Gehrig's disease. How do you feel? What changes when you put yourself into other roles like that of Jolly's son, doctor, or wife?

5

The Grief of Loss

L ittle Tex Allen was born to succeed, reared in a family of strong men, or so it seemed.[1] With a horse-trailer business bringing the American dream to the Allens, the neighbors and church folk saw them as the model family. But behind closed doors lay a mountain of unhealed wounds, a mass of pain which shook loose into an avalanche of grief with a simple phone call one afternoon.

"Daddy's had a stroke!" Tex's sister whimpered in an uncharacteristic panic. "Can you fly back from New Mexico? Help us make decisions? The doctors say he may not last the week." As Little Tex headed to the airport, his mind began to swirl with memories. Bolting from home at seventeen, Tex Allen had buried himself in his work, staying too busy to mourn the loss of his childhood. But as he flew silently over the West Texas mountains, he knew that his literacy work among Hispanic refugees, while good, had become a diminishing quick fix, no longer anesthetizing his past sorrows.

Objective and Subjective Losses

Tex and his family could count their share of losses, some old, some new, some publicly known, some kept in the closet of private thoughts. On some matters the whole family could agree: the patriarch was dying and life would never be the same. Familiar support systems of hospital, church, and community would offer some comfort too on this level. But Little Tex was struggling with those losses known only in the eyes of the beholder: the loss of safety (growing up with a harshly rejecting, perfectionistic father), the loss of trust (being molested by an alcoholic uncle in the barn, while his father slumbered nearby, too drunk to know or care), and the loss of a dream (no longer believing that if you just keep trying hard enough, life would work out and people would love you).

Coping with Loss

As the events unfolded in that final week of Big Tex Allen's life, Little Tex began seeing his family through thirty-year-old eyes, not through the lens of adolescent immaturity. He could see how his baby sister was torturing herself in a psychological purgatory, blaming herself for failing to get her stubborn father to stop smoking years before to avoid this stroke. If only she had tried harder! Her guilt let her stay in emotional contact with the man who could now only speak in single syllables.

Similarly Little Tex could not understand how his middle brother, lost in the competitiveness of the clan, had become the black sheep, orchestrating his own kind of negative attention. Even during this week, that brother's delinquency in the bedside routine shouted silent anger in indirect eloquence. And Mother, saint of all saints, was most obviously the smothering martyr whose co-dependence had been refined by years of singing harmony to a rage-addicted husband.

Tragically Mrs. Allen's denial had blinded her to the painful losses her children had suffered over the years, sucking virtually all of her nurturing energy into the black hole of overcompensation for an impossible man. In fact it began to make sense to Tex that by developing so much caregiving muscle in this troubled family, he was a natural for his high stress, on call, idealistic life's work. Amid the impossible challenges of refugee relief, Little Tex's hypervigilance had mushroomed into his own addiction to work.

Differentiation and the Battle for Identity

In the process of healing, Little Tex became acutely aware of differentiation, the process by which people determine how similar or dissimilar they will be to the significant others in their life. Rather than living in a world of borrowed identities, Tex determined to discover and absorb some of the qualities of his dying father and to yearn for a better caregiver balance than his "religious" mother had yet achieved.

In the closure of this final week Little Tex admitted that by trying to cut himself off from his family of shame, he had only welded himself to archaic perceptions, anchoring his identity in an obsolescent past. Through belabored conversation at the bedside and parallel reflections with his aunt, Little Tex came to learn that Big Tex, in his own odd way, had been proud of him for his work with the immigrants. The harsh threat to cut this son out of the will had been masculine babble from a man too proud to nurture.

Fortunately for the Tex Allens in all of us, there is One who is familiar with suffering (Isa. 53:3), aware of both our objective hurts as well as our subjective losses. The Lord himself gives us the potential to cope with these kinds of grief through his undiminished hope and love (Jer. 29:11; Lam. 3:32), propelling us on a supernatural trajectory toward the highest identity (Rom. 8:28–30; 1 John 3:2–3). By his grace, then, we move out to minister comfort amid the epidemic of unhealed grief wounds.[2] In this chapter it will be our purpose to understand the process of grief as well as to specify guidelines for healing the pain of grief.

Understanding the Process of Grief

Constructing a balanced view of grief will require insight from the Bible, augmented by observations from the behavioral sciences.

Biblical Insights for Understanding Grief

The Bible dignifies grief by presenting it as a God-given, therapeutic response to loss.

God grieves

The Father grieves over evil in Noah's day (Gen. 6:6)

The Son grieves over the death of Lazarus (John 11:35–38)

The Spirit grieves over believers' sin (Eph. 4:30)

God responds to our grief

Recording our tears (Ps. 56:8)

Sympathizing with our weaknesses (Heb. 4:15–16)

Eventually ending our griefs (Isa. 65:19; Rev. 21:4)

Grief measures the meaning of our attachments
    Our attachment to friends (John 11:36)
    Our attachment to family (Gen. 50:1)

Grief potentially interrupts life's routines
    Leaving mourners with little appetite (2 Sam. 12:17)
    Causing mourners to wish for death (2 Sam. 18:33)
    Multiplying mourners' illness and death (1 Sam. 4:18–22)

Grief potentially persists over an extended period of time
    For seven days (Gen. 50:10)
    For thirty days (Num. 20:29)
    For seventy days (Gen. 50:3)

Grief is potentially expressed in a variety of ways
    Before a loss (Matt. 26:37–38)
    By shock, numbness, or denial (Mark 8:31–32)
    In anger (Job 10:9)
    Through bargaining (Isa. 38:1–22)
    With depression (2 Sam. 12:16–18)
    With acceptance (Phil. 1:12, 21–24; 4:11–13)

Grief is potentially facilitated by artistic vehicles
    Through songs (2 Sam. 1:17–27)
    Through poetry (Lam. 1–5)

Psychosocial Insights for Understanding Grief

The six-year-old stands at the window, longing for her daddy to return from work so that he might rescue her from the man who kisses and touches her, making her promise not to tell. But her father will never return;

he was killed in a work accident over a year ago. So she keeps her vigil at the window.[3]

What has this little girl lost and for what does she grieve? Is there a part of her which is dead now? Can it ever come back to life? To augment the biblical insights into grief and to analyze this child's sorrow, we will consider four psychosocial subtopics in loss: the terms, types, timing, and transcendence of loss.

Terminology for loss and grief. To further clarify the grief process, we distinguish loss and grief. Loss is anything that seems to reverse or destroy a part of life, whereas grief is anything that seeks to measure the extent of a loss.

Types of loss and grief. Though loss is largely defined by the individual (as it is for the six-year-old) most people try to classify their losses. By coming up with a rational pigeonhole in which to place their setback, these people have created some sense of boundaries on their loss. By putting conceptual limits on the unwanted reversal, they have gained a small sense of control over it. Chicken Little's proverbial sky is no longer falling. To limit and classify their losses, most people use a series of comparisons.[4]

Major vs. Minor Loss

   A woman is raped vs.

   A woman's purse is stolen

Primary vs. Secondary Loss

   A person gets multiple sclerosis vs.

   A person has to give up jogging

Actual vs. Threatened Loss

   A bank teller is shot vs.

   A bank teller has a gun waved in his face

Internal vs. External Loss
  A spouse feels unloved vs.
  A spouse is sued for divorce
Chosen vs. Imposed Loss
  An employee resigns from a job vs.
  An employee is fired
Direct vs. Indirect Loss
  A child undergoes an operation vs.
  A child's parents watch helplessly

Though the six-year-old is unable to label her losses with precision, she has an instinctive sense that she is undergoing a major destruction of life. Until she is able to believe that her losses were externally imposed on her, she'll battle with false guilt and depression.

Timing in loss and grief. In addition to learning how people variably define and classify their losses, we must also weigh the impact of timing. Losing her dad and her innocence before the age of six, this first-grader has been left trying to learn the timing of social expectations by reading a shattered clock. Accordingly there seem to be three dimensions of time that affect our sense of loss.[5]

On-Time Loss: a normative transition that is expected and that comes on time
    Example: Graduating from college and giving up room and board being paid for by parents
    Losses of this type may surprise us if we have only anticipated gains; however, this type of loss is generally less devastating because of preparatory rehearsals and available support systems.

Off-Time Loss: a normative transition that is expected to occur, but at some other time

> Examples: a child dies; forced retirement before pension eligibility
>
> Losses of this type are usually more devastating than on-time ones.[6]

Time-Irrelevant Loss: a non-normative transition that was not expected

> Examples: Being raped; being in a serious accident or natural disaster
>
> Losses of this type are usually more difficult to overcome than normative losses.

An illustration may help crystallize these three types of time-related losses.[7] A couple may grieve over their children leaving the nest by age twenty to pursue school, marriage, or career goals (an on-time loss). But this same couple probably grieves more intensely when their married son informs them a decade later that their granddaughter was killed in a car accident (an off-time loss). Yet this couple's pain reaches its climax when they discover that this married son is an alcoholic and has been charged with vehicular manslaughter for causing the accident while driving while intoxicated (time-irrelevant loss). In time this couple's time-irrelevant losses may pile up if the daughter-in-law divorces the son and denies the grandparents visitation.

Transcending loss and grief. Finally, having weighed the impact of timing on the quality of grief, we will identify common methods people use to transcend loss. In general, people have tried to overcome their losses, using these methods.[8]

Direct action to change a stressor
   Examples: Finding another job; dating and remar-
   rying

Indirect action to change the meaning of the stressor
   Examples: Remembering some of the unpleasant
   realities that existed with the lost job or lost mate;
   making negative comparisons: "It could be worse,
   if . . ."

Substantive complexity to change the self
   Examples: Starting a new and better business for
   oneself and one's employees; committing oneself
   to becoming a better husband and father; developing a new faith in God and his ways

These methods involve altering the external environment, altering the inner climate, and altering the self,
respectively. As presented these methods involve a hier-
archy of coping styles which range from lesser to
greater in therapeutic value.

The little girl searching for her father at the window
is making an attempt to alter the external environment:
finding her father so he can protect her. Unfortunately it
will require a different outside intervention before the
abusive behavior stops and before her personal growth
and emotional healing can begin.

Healing from the Pain of Grief

Following a devastating fire in Boston some years
ago, a psychiatrist began working with survivors of the
tragedy as well as with relatives of the deceased. Surprised by the different rates at which people healed
from the catastrophe and surprised that some never
healed at all, the therapist suggested that there are cer-

tain processes in which a grieving person must engage to heal from loss, prompting the phrase "grief work."[9]

Once a loss has taken place and the grieving person has resolved to heal, there is a three-fold prescription that must be applied to the grief wound. When the bereaved actively engage in these three processes, they move steadily toward greater healing of their grief wounds. To illustrate the process, two metaphors can be used.

The medical metaphor. *First, a wound must be cleansed with the clean water of truth (making a realistic assessment).* Just as a doctor would flush a deep laceration with fresh water to remove any dirt that could lead to infection, so the grief wound must be washed of its inaccurate facts and faulty perceptions. Grieving people must confront their losses realistically, not only admitting to the wound but also revisiting the wound often enough to see it in the light of raw honesty. A complicated injury may even require the X-rays of a skillful counselor before it is fully assessed. False guilt, disproportionate anger, and unfounded anxiety must be cleansed before they triply infect the wound.

Second, the wound must be covered with the loving bandages of others (sharing the grief feelings). After the wound is cleansed, it must be wrapped with antiseptic gauze to prevent undue bleeding and reinfection. This step usually requires the wounded person to summon other caring people into an alliance for help. Few of us can bandage ourselves properly, and we dare not leave our wounds negligently vulnerable to new complications. Friends and loved ones can share the grief feelings with us, monitoring the healing process and giving us support with the tasks that seem too painful for the wounded limb.

Third, the wounded area must be rehabilitated by taking new risks in due time and in the proper environment (reinvesting in life). Although denial might keep a wounded person from having the injury cleansed and bandaged, morbid preoccupation could keep a person from rehabilitative therapy. Although the denial might keep a person from getting off the hurt leg, morbid preoccupation could prevent the retesting and restrengthening of the leg. For the person recovering from a compound-complex fracture, it is important to cleanse the wound, reset the bone, and support it in a cast. But if the injured person exaggerates the destruction of the leg or thrives on the borrowed identity of the cast and crutches, this person may atrophy in bed rather than selectively rebuild the use of the injured leg. With this kind of morbid preoccupation, the griever may lose far more life than necessary from the original injury. Although the one who has purposed to heal cannot presumptuously sign up for a marathon the day the cast comes off, numerous other challenges permit a responsible retraining of the wounded limb. It is even possible to work diligently enough at reinvesting in life that the injured limb becomes stronger at the end of rehabilitation than it was before the original accident.

The metaphor of healing a wound fits Paul's medical language for healing a wounded brother (Gal. 6:1). Just as with a physical or emotional wound, the spiritually injured Christian must make a realistic assessment (Luke 22:31–34; 1 John 1:9), share grief feelings (Luke 22:61–62), and begin reinvesting in life (John 21:15–17).

In addition to the clinical image of healing from a grief wound, the traveling metaphor also fits the motif of the pilgrim pressing ahead from the painful past.

The traveling metaphor. First of all, as pilgrim travelers we must realistically discover where we are. Before we can travel ahead, we must use an accurate map to give us our bearings. Before Moses could lead the Israelites toward Canaan, he had to know where Egypt was in relation to Canaan. Likewise those faced with loss must realistically identify where they are. They have to test the facts and revise the perceptions of their memories. In this regard, the apostle Paul was realistic; he was in a Roman prison. The patriarch Joseph was realistic; his father was dead. The Lord was realistic; he was going to the cross.

Second, as pilgrim travelers we must share the work with fellow sojourners. Moses couldn't carry all the baggage and herd all the animals from Egypt to Canaan. He had to share the work with others who were traveling the same path. Likewise those faced with loss must share the feelings of grief with others who care. In this same sense the apostle Paul shared his feelings about imprisonment with the Philippian church and their emissary, Epaphroditus (Phil. 2:25). Joseph wept with his family and friends for his father. Jesus prayed tearfully in Gethsemane, seeking support from his disciples but instead being comforted by an angel.

Third, as pilgrim travelers we must purpose to go on. Moses challenged his people to cross the Jordan despite the frightening giants in the land. The Israelites had to trust the Lord just as sincerely to enter Canaan as they had to exit Egypt. Likewise those faced with loss must choose to move ahead and to reintegrate with life now that the loss has occurred. Paul became content and revised his definition of the mission field by becoming an inmate ambassador to the Roman soldiers. Similarly Joseph obeyed his father's last wish for burial in Canaan and requested that his own bones be carried back to Canaan too. Jesus likewise accepted the cup and purposed to receive God's deliverance *through* the cross, not *from* the cross.

Reaching Out to Grievers

Having identified the essential tasks for our own healing from grief, we must not overlook the many walking wounded around us. In our increasingly fragmented society, grief has taken on crisis dimensions as people have lost their deep connection with family, community, and God.[10] But those equipped with a genuine faith will manifest a spiritual resiliency, enabling them to accept their finiteness because they have one foot firmly planted in the Infinite for eternity (1 Thess. 4:13–18).[11]

Vivian White was a person with a deep connectedness to the Infinite. Though we hoped she'd be able to win her third battle against cancer, we had our doubts. At eighty-four years of age and barely a hundred pounds, Mrs. White was staring at a very pessimistic prognosis.

Never able to bear children, this stalwart warrior had been left alone after the death of her mother and husband. Her crime-ridden neighborhood had locked her into her own house as if she were its lone prisoner.

Once home from the hospital, Mrs. White fought a lot longer and a lot harder than anyone expected she would. By gardening her potted plants, she had colorful gifts for her visitors and therapy for herself. Despite her trials, Mrs. White developed a prayer ministry that far excelled the average believer.

As the pain and disability increased, a niece moved a thousand miles across country to join Vivian in the last stages of her final journey. With the niece's arrival Mrs. White was able to remain at home where she wanted to be. And once the stairways became unscalable, the dining room was refashioned into a bedroom. When the pain became unbearable, morphine let her sleep.

Every effort was made to respect Mrs. White's desire for independence. When she wanted new locks on her doors, church friends installed them. Letting her pay for the locks and letting her order up crabcake sandwiches for the workmen showed she still had her dignity. It didn't matter that Mrs. White couldn't eat the crabcakes; it lifted her spirits to be the provider again.

Her recurring dream reminded us of her fierce desire for autonomy. With the morphine's help, she kept dreaming that there was a casket in her living room. When we realized that Mrs. White was feeling rushed to hurry up and die, we assured her that it was her body, her disease, and her house! No one was going to rush her. The dream soon disappeared.

At the time of her final diagnosis, Mrs. White's sadness focused on being childless. As a young minister I let her adopt me; after all, I needed a grandmother. As soon as she could, Mrs. White plastered pictures of our family around her house and began praying in earnest for our family.

On one visit, our three-year-old finished his concert and promptly began a search-and-destroy mission around the living room. Slithering on hands and knees, my boy soldier peeled off his RYAN sticker from his jacket. Attaching it to the bottom of some chair, he forgot where it was, destining us to leave Mrs. White's home stickerless.

Weeks later, the sticker was spotted stuck to the bottom of a chair. "Perfect," Mrs. White popped up. "Give it here!" Knowing immediately where it belonged, she pinned it on the door frame of her dining-room-turned-bedroom. There in her prayer chamber, she could remember to pray daily for Ryan and for his dad.

Until that final evening when Mrs. White took her last breath, the sticker stayed there. After laying this saint in the grave, I brought home that RYAN sticker to a boy who knew just where to put it. Pinning it on the wall beside his bed, he proudly grinned: "Every time I see this sticker, I'll remember my friend, Mrs. White, in heaven!"

The final months of Mrs. White's life are a story worth telling, not simply because of the many losses and griefs strewn on her pilgrim path, but because of her courage to move ahead on that sovereignly designed course. Though her life was full of objective and subjective losses, Vivian White learned to cope by the grace of God, ever emerging as the truly differentiated individual she was. Through her time-wisened understanding of the grief process, she saw with realism the journey that lay ahead of her, engaged in an active partnership to share the work of the trek, and kept putting one foot in front of the other, investing in each tomorrow until she crossed over Jordan.

Discussion Questions

1. Choose a book, poem, TV show, or movie and analyze its teachings about aging, grief, and death. Pay attention to objective and subjective losses, coping styles, and differentiation.
2. Which of Tex Allen's experiences are most similar to yours? Most different from yours? How would you help Little Tex? Big Tex? Mrs. Allen? The brother and sister?
3. In what ways does our culture teach that grief is suitable only for women and children? What are the consequences of such teaching and what can you do about it?

4. Which biblical insight about grief was most helpful to you? Least helpful? Why?

5. Which psychosocial insight about grief was most helpful to you? Least helpful? Why?

6. Analyze the losses of the six-year-old who was keeping vigil at the window and compare them to the losses of her mother.

7. Which of the tasks for overcoming loss and grief come most easily for you? Why? Most difficult? Why?

8. What are the strengths and weaknesses of the medical and traveling metaphors? Identify at least one more metaphor and correlate it to the grief process.

9. Why is genuine faith so crucial in our society as we seek to cope with grief and loss?

10. Reread the story of Mrs. White in light of the principles of this chapter. List the correlations you discover.

6

The Pain of Suicide

Friends, it is my great pleasure tonight to introduce to you my brother, the Reverend Donald Gates.[1] Donald and I were orphaned as teens, the only son and daughter of a West Virginia coal-mining couple. But despite our parents' untimely deaths, God saved both of us and sent us into religious vocations for him. With Donald in the pastorate and me on the mission field, we never felt like orphans. To the contrary, we felt like we had been adopted into a larger spiritual family, the family of God.

"As you know, my brother and his wife are vacationing from their busy ministry in Scottsdale, Arizona. There Reverend Gates founded First Christian Church three decades ago, leading to a twelve-hundred member congregation with a multiple staff today. Alongside her husband, Mrs. Gates also has her ministry of women's retreats and Bible studies. In fact her teaching gifts have proven themselves far beyond the walls of the church, leading her to become a highly recognized pedagogy specialist in the public school system.

"Donald's subject tonight, Everyday Evangelism, has been a standing priority for him over the years. He is involved in training the average person in the pew to reach out with his or her faith. In fact as he looks ahead to retirement within the next couple of years he hopes to devote himself to writing gospel tracts and doing Everyday Evangelism seminars in churches like ours. And so let's welcome my big brother and friend, the Reverend Donald Gates to the pulpit of Memorial Baptist Church."

Less than two years after the polite applause had ended, Donald took his life. Looping two leather belts together, this once-successful pastor hanged himself from his staircase railing. Within the hour of his fatal choice, in the lobby of the house where church friends had often greeted, Mrs. Gates was met by an ashen corpse dangling in the stillness of death. After a brief flurry of fruitless rescue activity, this widow was left with that final scene burned into her memory by the acid of emotional panic.

If Donald had been murdered or killed in a car accident, his death would have been easier to accept. If that last scene had been a sick joke or a passing nightmare, Mrs. Gates would have healed quickly. If this man of the cloth had succumbed to cancer or a heart attack there would have been no stigma. But Donald Gates was dead by suicide.

Though the chaos of grief would spawn a kaleidoscope of reactions, Donald Gates' psychological autopsy would begin making sense out of the unimaginable. As an elderly white male Donald was in the high-risk group for potential suicide. As often happens with men like him, retirement came with the same devastation as bereavement might to a widow. Forever gone was his youthfulness, his financial productivity, and his job-centered identity. After retiring he had apparently slipped into an undiagnosed depression that worsened for a year and a half—a depression that left unrecognized but telltale signs along its path to self-destruction.

As a perfectionist Donald couldn't bring himself to ask for help and so he kept all of his feelings inside, gradually dying in private. After serving many years as the gifted professional, he knew he should have the answers. Furthermore his trademark idealism led him to expect that in his retirement years he would become a published author and a fairly sought-after speaker. When neither developed, his retirement income proved embarrassingly slim while his wife's work was taking off exponentially. Without children or grandchildren to receive his love, Donald's rigid role-break from the church only aided the publication of his obituary.

With the same aching curiosity that drove Mrs. Gates to seek insight from a suicide counselor, this chapter will ask and answer three questions: *How common is the problem of suicide? Why do people commit suicide? What can we do to prevent suicide?*

How Common Is the Problem of Suicide?

For those who have never been tempted to kill themselves nor been shocked by the self-destructive bent of a loved one, it is important to look at suicide realistically. To help in sizing up the problem, we will look at the commonness of suicide in the Bible, the patterns of suicide during the teen and adult years, and the characteristics of suicide in statistical profile.

Suicide in the Bible

The Bible records seven suicides: Abimelech (Judg. 9:54), Samson (Judg. 16:30), King Saul (1 Sam. 31:4), Saul's armor-bearer (1 Sam. 31:5), Ahithophel (2 Sam. 17:23), Zimri (1 Kings 16:18), Judas (Matt. 27:5). Throughout the Word of God, plants and animals never elect to end life. Rather God's noblest creatures (Gen. 1:26–29), aware of their frustrated potentialities, make the fatal choice with deadly frequency.

Suicide During the Teen Years[2]

During the teen years, adult-size problems meet child-size maturity, resulting in myriad self-inflicted deaths. Statistics released in 1988 said that every year in America, six thousand teenagers kill themselves and more than six hundred thousand try. Further complicating the problem, families and public officials tend to disguise teen suicides as accidents, leading some experts to estimate the annual teen suicide count at twenty thousand. With the rate of teenage suicide tripling over the last thirty years, the story of cluster suicides has become a contagious sensation spot for the nightly news.

According to specialists, a million children move in and out of suicidal crises, thoughts, and episodes every year in the USA, leaving one out of every ten students at risk at any given time. Furthermore, with child suicide occurring at younger ages, the threat of a nine- or ten-year-old committing suicide becomes a very real possibility.

Suicide During the Adult Years[3]

Even for adults who have survived the teen years, an active suicide vigil must never be ruled out. Every year thirty thousand adults become official suicide statistics, with as many as seventy thousand additional suicides masked or misreported as accidents. Tragically the annual suicide rate continues to rise steadily as it has for nearly two decades.

Suicide is one of the top ten causes of adult death in the USA.

Suicide is the number two cause of death for young adults 15–24.

Suicide attempts and suicide completions increase with age.

Suicide will be considered by eight out of every ten people.

Suicide survivors number over 2 million and many will try again.

Autocide accounts for 5 percent of the deaths in single-car-accidents.

To make these demographics personal, let's imagine inviting one hundred thousand typical adults to fill a large football stadium. Within a year of the game, fifteen to forty people in the assemblage, depending on the average age in the crowd, would officially commit suicide. More than ten times that number would attempt suicide and double that number would kill themselves but it would be labeled "accidental." In the fatal crowd, five out of six attempters would be women; but three out of four completers would be men. For every black suicide in the group, there would be three whites. For every nonprofessional, white-collar worker in the suicidal group, there would be three times as many doctors, dentists, and lawyers and four times as many psychiatrists.

Profile of Suicide Characteristics[4]

The characteristics of those who are more likely to *attempt* suicide include:

Young
Female
Married
Personality disordered

Experiencing a domestic crisis

Facing a personal relationship problem

Most of us can identify with several of these characteristics at some time in our life.

Those most likely to *complete* suicide include:

Male

Senior adult and baby boomer

Unmarried, married young, widows, divorced, bored
   housewife

Living alone and unemployed

Poor physical health

Severe emotional pain and feeling helpless to express
   it

Alcohol and drug abuse

Perfectionistic

Learning disabled

Early separation from parents

Dysfunctional family of origin

Excessively high expectations from parents

Relationally escapist, manipulative, and attention
   seeking

Previous suicide attempt and parent who committed
   suicide

Exposed to violence in family and media and Vietnam

During winter months and Christmas season and
   April

Protestants

Urban lifestyle and apartment dweller

Glamor States: Nevada, California, Florida

Young American Indians

Very poor and very rich

Despite the predictive nature of these profiles, even one suicide is too many. And no "I-told-you-so!" has ever brought a loved one back.

Why Do People Commit Suicide?

Although self-destruction will always be surrounded by a well-deserved aura of irrationality, there nonetheless are familiar patterns surrounding it, patterns which offer potential insight. With a view to understanding these causes of suicide, two common paradigms will be surveyed, leading to a third and more integrated proposal.

The Psychiatric Paradigm[5]

The psychiatric paradigm presupposes that people kill themselves because they suffer from some inner emotional disorder.

Psychosis: a gross inability to perceive reality
    Example: paranoid schizophrenia
Neurosis: an unusual degree of subjective distress with life
    Example: obsessive-compulsive disorders
Personality disturbances: habitual maladaptive behavior
    Example: alcoholism
Depression: profound sadness
    Example: manic depression

When rethinking the case of Donald Gates, one can identify his depression, his obsessive perfectionism, and his possible work addiction, all feeding his suicidal tendency.

The Sociological Paradigm[6]

The sociological paradigm presupposes that people kill themselves because of external stressors.

Religious alienation
  Example: being excommunicated or detached from one's church
Domestic alienation
  Example: being separated from one's parents, spouse, children
Political alienation
  Example: being rejected by one's national or partisan group

Again Reverend Gates can be seen as a man struggling with his sense of belonging, no longer the caring professional in charge of a congregation. Instead he discovers himself as the failed breadwinner, sitting idly at home while his wife grabs for the brass ring of success now beyond his reach. Having spent his pastoral years critiquing every sociopolitical movement from atop his separatistic soapbox, he now finds himself a man without a cause.

The Holistic Paradigm

In addition to the foregoing paradigms, we cannot fail to mention the parallel spiritual factors in suicide as well. According to one pastoral specialist, suicide is a "tactic foisted upon mankind by the darkest side of the spiritual world, a hand grenade out of the pit of hell."[7]

One's degree of stress interplays with one's degree of competency, as shown in Chart 2.[8] Needless to say we can experience stress both within ourselves (the psychiatric paradigm) as well as outside ourselves (the sociological paradigm). Furthermore we can meet our stres-

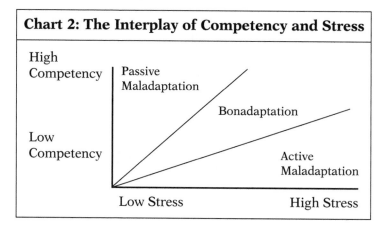

Chart 2: The Interplay of Competency and Stress

High
Competency | Passive Maladaptation

Bonadaptation

Low
Competency

Active Maladaptation

Low Stress   High Stress

sors with coping resources that are primarily within (the former paradigm), while others are primarily without (the latter paradigm). However, we must broaden the framework for competencies and stressors so that it also includes the spiritual dimension, leaving us with an integrated model of the biopsychospiritual life (1 Thess. 5:23).

Donald Gates lived out an interplay of stresses that were both within (perfectionism) and without (financial pressures). Furthermore he failed to meet these stressors competently, either to draw on the grace of God inwardly or to engage a retirement counselor who could bring support from the outside.

In looking at the holistic interplay of competency and stress, we might consider altruistic suicide as bonadaptive (the soldier who throws himself on a live grenade to save five comrades). Anomic suicide could be seen as actively maladaptive (a disgruntled employee who goes out in a blaze of glory, killing himself and his boss), while egoistic suicide would correspond to passive maladaptation (Donald Gates's hanging himself because he deserved better in life).

Did Jesus commit suicide? It seems evident from Jesus' self-stated motives and actions (John 10:10–18) that he did not commit anomic or egoistic suicide, forms of maladaptive behavior. If a case were to be made for Jesus' death as a suicide, it would have to be for the altruistic type of elective death. However even this idea is excluded by definition since "suicide is a self-inflicted, self-intentioned death."[9] Since Jesus' death was clearly inflicted by others, it cannot be considered a suicide in the classic sense.

Theologians, such as Augustine, have argued that suicide is the unpardonable sin (Matt. 12:31), destining people like Judas to hell (John 17:12; Matt. 27:5). Reasoning that this apostle was guilty of self-murder, they contend that Judas could never have been forgiven after death since his suicide would have kept him from having the necessary time to do penance. Although this logic is not scriptural, it has been powerful. Even into the 1800s, people who committed suicide in England had a stake driven through the heart, were buried outside of consecrated ground, and had their goods confiscated by the government. In fact until the mid-1900s, the majority of Christian traditions forbade funerals for people who had killed themselves.[10]

If we are going to truly help people affected by suicide, we will need to spend energy preventing the lethal depletion of hope, intervening in the lonely momentum of fatal thinking, and redirecting life for bereaved survivors.

How Can Suicide Be Prevented?

Of the hundreds who leap to their death from the Golden Gate Bridge each year, nearly all jump facing San Francisco.[11] Since very few jump facing the Pacific Ocean, there seems to be, even in death, an orientation toward people. This same orientation provides subtle hope that we might be able to influence those who are contemplating suicide. A loving family or church may prove to be the difference between coping or collapsing.

A common form of suicide-prevention centers around short-term care for those at risk. Calling a hotline or visiting a suicide-prevention center is believed to reduce one's lethality index for suicide. Another form of suicide-prevention centers around the cultivation of healthy thinking. To further such thinking, suicidologists have challenged myths with facts.[12]

Myths Surrounding Suicide

Myth 1: People who talk about suicide don't complete the act.

Fact: About 75 percent of those who attempt suicide have communicated their intentions ahead of time.

Myth 2: When a suicidal person improves, the danger has passed.

Fact: The upswing in mood may indicate that a decision has finally been reached, yielding sufficient energy to carry out the plan. Many suicides occur within three to six months of the worst depression.

Myth 3: Once people are at risk, they are always at risk.

Fact: The longer a person with suicidal thinking can be denied the means of death or treated with crisis intervention, the more the risk diminishes.

Myth 4: Suicide is inherited.

Fact: Suicide is not genetically determined; but people do influence each other.

Myth 5: Suicide affects only a specific group or class of people.

Fact: Suicide occurs among all socioeconomic and lifestyle groups.

Myth 6: Suicidal behavior is insane.

Fact: While some suicides are sourced in mental illness, most suicide notes and acts require considerable lucidity.

Myth 7: Suicidal people are 100 percent convinced they want to die.

Fact: Most attempters are ambivalent, fantasizing about rescue; only 5–10 percent will ultimately succeed; attempts are often a form of communication.

Myth 8: The motive for a particular suicide can be easily determined.

Fact: Although causes will be quickly attributed, prolonged patterns of self-destructive behavior may require specialized analysis.

Handling Suicide Threats

When we hear someone speak of suicide, we should take the threat seriously, moving them toward detoxification (if drugs or alcohol are involved) and recovery. Further we should compassionately inquire to see if the person considering suicide has a specific plan in mind. In addition we should explore current feelings, suicidal history, and problem-solving alternatives. Finally we must be sure to create an accountability system, possibly soliciting help from professional interventionists (the police or rescue squad).

To redirect the suicidal person's deadly momentum toward destiny, it is critical for us to understand their rationale for suicide.[13] For some suicide is the great death, the final dramatic curtain call. For others it seems to be the rational alternative, the reunion with a loved one, the escape from pain, the revenge of an injustice, or one's due punishment.

Telephone hotline services to handle emergencies are springing up around the country. Generally these services are staffed by volunteers, supervised by a mental-health professional. The phones are open twenty-four hours a day, callers are allowed to remain anonymous, and the need for help is accepted unquestioningly. Counsel includes stress reduction, problem solving, and a possible referral for a face-to-face appointment.

Standard practice in suicide counseling will explore ambivalence, brainstorming the apparent pros and cons of the contemplated action. Further intervention will seek to identify new options for problem solving that were beyond the awareness of the troubled person. While some interventionists would negotiate a suicide contract to buy time for the distressed person, others would send the ambulance immediately, allowing a hospitalization to more safely accomplish the same purpose. For all of us, whether suicidal or otherwise, God's love refreshes the weary soul (Matt. 11:28–30).

Nate, a young man with a tender conscience, hitchhiked all the way from Boston to Niagara Falls with a plan: to commit suicide over the falls. But in the wisdom of God, a tourist stopped him and told him of the love of Christ. For Nate the news of Jesus Christ was truly the good news of life and death.

Suicide Postvention

Though an actual suicide can never be undone after the fact, there is nevertheless a tendency to punish the deceased through the doctrine of unpardonability or through burying the person's life in the silence of a family secret. In the Middle Ages a person who had committed suicide would be tried in court, declared guilty of a crime, and exhumed from consecrated ground. In some cases the deceased was then buried in a cemetery surrounded by a wall with no doors, leaving the grave diggers to pass the coffin over the boundary.[14]

More realistically modern postvention seeks to discover why a particular suicide has taken place, using an assessment procedure called the psychological autopsy. Sadly these diagnostic methods often reveal from hindsight what might have been lifesaving had it been noticed in time. One college student, for example, felt devoid of friends and took his life, leaving his body undiscovered in a dorm room for eighteen days; nobody missed him. The psychological autopsy revealed that he felt friendless, he had no one to turn to, no one who cared about him.[15]

In addition to the psychological autopsy, modern postvention also seeks to help survivors put their lives back together. A suicide, hanging a psychological skeleton in the closet, often persecutes loved ones with the burning question: "What could I have done to prevent this?" But just as survivors might like to remind their beloved deceased that God never gives us more than we can bear (1 Cor. 10:13), so the survivor will have to rest on the same truth. The enormous guilt left over from another's suicide can drive a wedge between family or friends who find it easy to scapegoat themselves or each other. In every case God can cleanse, not only of legitimate guilt (1 John 1:9), but from the false guilt that could drown us (1 John 3:19–21). To truly recover each person involved must admit that no one, counselor or pastor included, can take full responsibility for the decisions of another person. It is a fact that even Emergency Room psychiatrists have a difficult time assessing the suicide potential of a patient.[16]

In the years after a suicide, survivors will replay the ninth inning thousands of times, plagued by their "What if?" But for those who have survived the tragedy, at least one positive potential still remains: to teach others the lessons of the past in an effort to save one more life today.

Steve, a teen suffering from the divorce of his parents, was being moved back and forth between family households. His dad, angered by the high schooler's deteriorating grades and mounting tardiness, called on the phone and screamed at the son. Intending to get Steve's guilt in gear, the father was planning to call back and repair the relationship, but only after his outburst would have had time to put Steve back on track. As the father now tells other parents, the method had worked before; he had no reason to doubt it then.

Unfortunately the boomerang effect of that first phone call would leave that dad with plenty to doubt. Within an hour of the first call, Steven completed his homework, attaching two notes to it. The notes, to his mother and father, revealed Steve's reaction to the phone conversation and to life.[17] In his note to his mother, the troubled teen apologized for "not being good enough" for her, describing himself as destined to hell for the sin of suicide. After drawing the teardrops, this anguishing adolescent admitted to "messing up the family," while offering his loving farewell to each one. In the aftermath of his grief, Steve's broken dad began rebuilding his life by helping parents learn the power of true parental love (Ps. 27:10; 1 John 3:18).

Discussion Questions

1. If you were conducting the psychological autopsy interviews with the Reverend Gates's family and friends, what questions would you ask?

2. When have you come closest to suicide? If you were considering it right now, what would you do to try to prevent it? How do you personally cultivate healthy thinking?

3. Reread the suicide profiles and the myth and fact list. What ones were most surprising?

4. Name several current stressors in your life related to having what you do not want or wanting what you do not have.

5. In your opinion did Jesus commit suicide? Is suicide the unpardonable sin?

6. Why do most suicides who jump off the Golden Gate Bridge face San Francisco? What does your answer suggest about suicide prevention and spiritual connectedness to the body of Christ?

7. How do you feel about Suicide-Prevention Centers putting their major efforts into interventive techniques rather than preventive education?

8. In what ways do we punish suicides today?

9. Why is it important to recognize that no person can take full responsibility for the actions of another?

10. What lessons do you believe Steve's dad learned from Steve's suicide? Is it healthy for him to be reaching out now to teens and their parents?

7

The Challenge of Aging

Do your best to come to me quickly," the elderly prisoner wrote as he closed his letter (2 Tim. 4:9a). Here sat a man, seasoned in trusting God but reaching out for help. The help he needed wasn't dramatic but it was real. The veteran missionary, Paul, was asking young Timothy for some simple things: a personal visit, his coat and scrolls, and a little help in reconciling his relationship with John Mark. Apparently as the apostle awaited his execution, he was doing his work of life review. With intense realism about the future, he was humble enough to ask for help. In loving simplicity, this high-powered statesman asked his son in the faith for some precious little commodities.

Though we only have record of Paul's requests in this exchange, Timothy's response is probably self-evident. Though no doubt surprised by the role reversal, Timothy would most assuredly have accepted his lot to care for his mentor. With mirror-image realism, Timothy refused to stereotype Paul as if the apostle were somehow incapable of needing help, instead coming before winter to meet the senior's practical needs (2 Tim. 4:21).

Like Timothy we all have beloved friends and family who face real challenges in the wintertime of their lives. If we are honest, our own aging demands that we face life with enough realistic humility to be able to ask for help. With these real-life eldercare relationships in mind, this chapter offers help to the aging Pauls and caregiving Timothys in modern times. For people like them we ask three questions: *How do we know we are aging? What are the challenges in aging?* And, *how can we overcome the challenges in aging?*

The Fact of Aging Confirmed

To realists it seems absurd to ask, "Are we aging?" But in a death-denying culture like ours, honest answers don't come easily. In a nation that freezes its dead in hopes of a cure, that masks aging with billions of cosmetic dollars, and that deifies medical scientists, we need honest answers. The affirmative answer to this troubling question comes to us from four sources: *the Bible, our bodies, our society, and our psyche.* In fourfold harmony, the melody of our lives resounds with the lone lyric that we are all aging.

In the Bible

In the oldest psalm of the Bible, a wise shepherd captured three basic realities of life: God is eternally strong (Ps. 90:1–2), man is sinfully weak (vv. 3–11), and grace is desperately needed (vv. 12–17).

Moses, perhaps presiding at a massive funeral for thousands of his wilderness kinsmen, described God as the eternal dwelling place. Neither Egypt, nor Midian, the wilderness, nor Canaan were enduring places to live. Instead God himself was the One in whom his people could abide (John 15:4–5)—a centering point for all generations. Like a parent present for the birth of a child, the eternal God had presided at the birth of the earth and the mountains. In contrast to his finite children, God remains forever unchanged.

Mortal man fulfills the Edenic edict; borrowed from the dust, each pays back the loan in due time. Even a Methuselan life is like yesterday when it is over, always irretrievable, easily slept through, like a watch in the night. God, being much less concerned about adding years to our life, concentrates on adding life to our years (John 10:10b), investing in a life of quality over quantity (1 Cor. 3:11–15). We are warned, lest we spend our lives trying to climb some ladder of success only to find when we arrive at the top that it is leaning against the wrong wall.

Our lives, described by Moses, are as cut grass. Like the browning of a mown meadow, our vitality is soon gone. Even a lengthy life can end with a sigh as quickly as a bird startling from its roost.

When we come to see our sinful transiency against the backdrop of God's eternity, it moves us to a reverent hunger for him to be the centering point of our lives. In renewed humility we ask for him to teach us that our earthly time clocks are running, to forgive us for our many sins, and to show us his enduring work. Without his gracious intervention, we would waste our days, sinning freely and idolizing our puny deeds.

In Our Bodies

On top of the Bible's clear warning that we are aging, our bodies also signal a progressive physical decline. Normal physical changes with age include:[1]

1. Cardiovascular stamina decreases 30 percent by age 70.

2. Muscle strength decreases 20 percent by age 70.
3. Rate of reflex slows 10 percent by age 70.
4. Height and shoulder breadth decreases 1 inch by age 70.
5. Weight increases 20 pounds from age 20–50, losing 6 from age 50–70; total body weight is 15 percent fat at age 20 and 30 percent by age 70.
6. Skin thins, becomes less elastic, and wrinkles.
7. Hairs decrease 20 percent in diameter by age 70; grays from reduction in pigment; whitens from loss of all pigment.
8. Nails decrease in growth rate 30 percent by age 70.
9. Ten teeth are lost by age 70.
10. Vision requires reading glasses and glare protection by age 50; greens and blues almost indistinguishable by age 60; peripheral and night vision diminished by age 70.
11. Skull bone thickens; cranial circumference increases; nose and earlobes become longer and wider.
12. Taste buds decrease 65 percent by age 70; mouth is drier.
13. Voice pitch rises and tremors more.
14. Brain loses neurons; timed IQ and short-term memory scores decrease 20 percent by age 70; sleep region affected.
15. Bones have less calcium, looser cartilage, harder ligaments, and less joint lubrication.
16. Kidney and bladder function decreases 50 percent by age 70.
17. Hearing misses higher pitches like S and T, making the words of others sound garbled.
18. Orgasm requires more time in foreplay; frequency of orgasm decreases.

19. Cholesterol increases 25 percent in the blood by age 70; blood pressure increases 20 percent over 15 percent by age 70.

Thus biological research agrees with the Word of God: we are aging. But even the eighty-two-year-old Dr. Seuss offered encouragement: "You are in pretty good shape for the shape you are in!"[2]

In Our Society

If we had somehow missed the wake-up call from the Bible and from our bodies, it would be hard to stay ignorant of aging's stern arrival. The society in which we live would rouse us to the realization that we are aging, even if others are permitted to deny their own. Forced retirement, Social Security qualification, insurance rates, and the reactions of others would signal that we are getting old.

In a society that receives the lion's share of its information and values through television, we would be wise to reflect on what our society says via this medium. With only 1 percent of prime-time characters being sixty-five or older (compared to 12 percent in the population), television suggests that the old are rare and probably lonely (whereas only 7 percent of the elderly describe themselves as lonely). With ads portraying the elderly as constipated, bald, and wrinkled, television suggests that seniors are bereft of health, joy, and productivity (whereas 75 percent of the elderly live healthy, independent lives). With negative trait clusters projected on fictional elders, males are stereotyped as dirty old men, females as weak and exploitable.

To stereotype the elderly on television would be like portraying blacks as street thugs, Italians as Mafia, attractive women as promiscuous, politicians as inept, or clergy as cult leaders. These caricatures contribute to widespread gerontophobia and condition the elderly to live out self-fulfilling prophecies. It is not surprising, then, that older adults who watch a lot of television become increasingly passive, manifesting a learned helplessness.

In Our Minds

Not only are we aware of our own aging because of the Word of God, because of our bodily changes, and because of the reactions of others toward us, but deep within we have an undeniable awareness that we are aging.

I am convinced that most of us eventually get stunned by looking in our psychological mirror and realizing how life has gotten away from us; aging has come before its time. The childhood disease, Progeria, manifests itself with characteristics of premature aging: baldness, thinning of the skin, prominence of surface blood vessels, and circulatory disorders, leaving children with this disease looking like little old men and dying in their teen years. Even without literal Progeria, we must be courageous to gaze into the mirror of self-awareness, staring until our initial sense of prematurity fades, etching our new mental image in stone. Such courage lets us step back into life, revising our values, and accepting our limitations accordingly.

One revision of values commonly promoted by this new honesty concerns eternal things. According to *The Gallup Report,* the spiritual commitment of Americans often grows as they age.[3]

View of Religion	Age 30–49	Age 50–64	Age 65+
Most important influence	67%	76%	82%
Gives personal comfort	77%	85%	87%
Try hard to practice	81%	86%	89%

Like the Bristlecone Pine which finds nourishment even on icy mountain peaks, the older adult with a vital spiritual dimension tenaciously adapts to life.[4]

Another result of this psychological honesty is to accept some cognitive limitations. Although our long-term memory and teachability remain constant, our short-term recall and pace of mental processing slows.

But although the absolute recall of fluid intelligence decreases, crystallized intelligence (the ability to use practical and time-tested knowledge) seems to improve. Although younger adults think more quickly, the senior adult thinks more accurately, hitting the nail on the head more often with wise thinking. Such wisdom replaces the youth-oriented trial and error logic of youth. And while our scientific achievements are more likely to occur while we are in our thirties, our experiential achievements in areas like politics, administration, and religion are more likely to occur after age sixty.[5]

The Challenges of Aging

It has been said that a problem well defined is half-solved. So if we are going to succeed in aging, we must define the two specific challenges which lie in our path: first, *to accept our new physical limitations* and, second, *to maintain an optimistic outlook on life.*

Adjust to New Physical Limitations

Solomon, the wise elder, defined some of the potential decremental changes in old age. In Ecclesiastes 12:3–5, the king wrote about the divinely created body, running down like a biological time clock for which the rewind key is now lost. Through this mosaic, he uses metaphors to describe a stoic aging trajectory:

Hands tremor
Posture stoops

Chewing decreases
Eyesight deteriorates
Mouth closes
Hearing diminishes
Sleep easily interrupted
High frequencies become less audible
Balance becomes more precarious
Hair grays or whitens
Physical movements become labored
Sexual response declines
Body dies

Similarly, a pessimistic Shakespeare wrote,

> Last scene of all,
> That ends this strange eventful history
> Is second childishness, and mere oblivion,
> Sans teeth, sans eyes, sans taste, sans everything.[6]

Although no individual will experience all of the decremental changes highlighted by Solomon and Shakespeare, these potential declines signal the priority for sound nutrition, exercise, rest, safety precautions, health care, and the setting of reasonable expectations.

But lest we think that all old people are unhappy, life-satisfaction research shows that older adults with the capacity to share love and enjoy work have the highest degree of well-being.[7]

Maintain an Optimistic Outlook on Life

Solomon not only defined the challenge of adjusting to new physical limitations (Eccles. 12:3–5), he also identified threats to our sense of security (Eccles. 12:1–2, 5):

Life seems troublesome and less pleasurable.

The autumn of life has come and winter is near.

Dangers become exaggerated.

With psychospiritual resolve adults must choose to cultivate an optimistic outlook on life.

Genuine optimism will be rooted in realistic faith, not panicky denial. Thus the woman of excellence can smile at the future because she is handling her todays well, harvesting an inward beauty that increases with age (Prov. 31:25; 1 Peter 3:3–5) and which enriches her world intergenerationally (Titus 2:3–4).

In 1934 Winston Churchill believed he was over the hill, but with courageous optimism, he continued serving his country and the free world for another twenty years. About this remarkable man a London newspaper described him on his seventieth birthday as a young man with a very bright future.

Meeting the Challenges of Aging

Just as the philosophic Solomon was guided by God to portray the physical and psychosocial challenges of aging (Eccles. 12:1–5), he also was inspired to give advice on how to meet those challenges in a godly way. The foundation of his advice is that we invest in knowing God throughout the lifespan; and on this foundation, God helps us lay practical building blocks of time-tested wisdom.

Know God

In the great geriatric chapter of the Bible, Solomon sends us back to the Creator of the body (Eccles. 12:1) who alone can prepare us for our final journey (v. 5b). Once the light and water of life are cut off (v. 6), the pilgrim body is buried while the eternal spirit returns to God (v. 7). At this doorway to eternity, only one epitaph will matter: that we obeyed God (vv. 13–14). And since God's compassions are new every morning, announcing a new day of salvation (Lam. 3:22–23; 2 Cor. 6:2), it is never too late to begin doing what is right, regardless of age.

Take Care of the Body

These bodies, given to us from the moment of conception, are a lifelong stewardship, eventually worthy of resurrection. But we often give in to decline, losing as much as half of our physical performance in older adulthood from disuse, not from disease.[8] To prevent an exaggerated decline, regular exercisers are finding that they not only generally outlive their sedentary peers, they have other rewards too: firmer muscles, less fat, stronger lungs, better balance, increased flexibility, and improved cardiovascular circulation. These advantages, in turn, build the older adult's self-esteem and independence, while at the same time reducing anxiety and depression.[9] The bottom line of human performance shows that a physically fit older adult thinks better than a physically unfit twenty-five-year-old.

Continue Lifelong Learning

"You can't teach an old dog new tricks!" How many times have we heard this worn-out stereotype, sabotaging the learning curve of senior adults? Beyond knowing God and taking care of the body, adults of all ages are capable of practicing lifelong learning. And thanks to geriatric educators, the caricature of the old dog can be replaced with a model for age-appropriate teaching.

"You Can't Teach an Old Dog New Tricks . . .

. . . if the dog refuses to learn" (resistant motivation)

. . . if the dog is convinced it's too ignorant to learn" (lowered self-concept)

. . . as fast as you could teach a young dog" (slowed response time)

. . . if the dog has hearing and/or vision deficits" (sensory handicaps)

Our culture further stifles older adult learning by dividing life into three mutually exclusive stages: childhood (a time for play and school), adulthood (a time for work), and retirement (a time for rest). By following this simplistically linear view of life, Americans think they are going against the cultural tide when teaching their children the ethic of hard work, when teaching their working adults the ethic of leisure, and when teaching their retirees the ethic of lifelong learning. A wiser lifestyle would interweave love, work, and play throughout the years.

To illustrate our healthier heritage, the church in colonial times placed a priority on educating adults, teaching them to read the Bible and to appreciate liberal studies and the performing arts. So as we minister to older adults today, we are likewise more effective if we view these seniors not primarily in terms of their chronological age, but through the potential richness of their life experience. And as we teach our older adults, we will seek to target the comprehensive educational needs listed below.[10]

Expressive Needs
Engaging in activities for inherent enjoyment
(a singspiration, using good old hymns)

Transcendence Needs
>   Achieving a sense of higher fulfillment
>   (a senior presence on church government board)

Coping Needs
>   Acquiring skills necessary in society
>   (senior safe-driving course)

Contributive Needs
>   Participating in service activities
>   (seniors as volunteer teachers in church education)

Influence Needs
>   Becoming an agent of social change
>   (senior involvement in community needs)

And as we facilitate formal learning programs for our older adults, we may sense a psychosocial tension stemming from the private world of our learners, a tension which requires them to seek transcendence if they wish not to become stagnantly preoccupied with the smaller issues of life.[11]

>   Work transcendence vs. work preoccupation
>   ("There's more to me than my formal job identity!")
>
>   Body transcendence vs. body preoccupation
>   ("There is more to me than how my body looks and feels!")
>
>   Ego transcendence vs. ego preoccupation
>   ("There is more to life than just me!")

As a whole, this kind of learning seeks to integrate the meaning of life and to prevent premature decline and rigidity.

To prove that the average older adult is no disinterested learner, research shows that retirees typically spend over three hundred hours per year in self-directed learning. Some, usually the urban upper class, spend two thousand hours per year investing in their ongoing growth.[12] And even beyond self-initiated study, a growing number of these adults enroll in organized educational programs, stimulating group learning and minimizing social isolation.

And the future of older adult education is even brighter if we can see "the new source of power as not being money in the hands of a few but information in the hands of many."[13] Toward this end, the university system is well on its way to becoming "a broadly organized effort to enable all members of society to learn where, when, what, and in the way that best suits them."[14]

Plan for Retirement

By knowing God, by taking care of the body, and by practicing lifelong learning, older adults buffer themselves against some of the hardships of their future. For many retirement comes as this kind of fracturing hardship. But what makes retirement so upsetting and what can be done to help the retiree?

There are a number of factors that make retirement difficult: boredom, loss of income, feelings of incompetence, undesirable exit scenarios from work, inadequate preparation for this transition, new territorial wars at home, and social expectations that retirement is a right but not a contributive role.

After retiring from the presidency, William Howard Taft felt this letdown from the retirement transition, describing himself in retirement as a "giant locomotive pulling a toy train."[15] And it is this kind of apparent meaninglessness that can haunt the retiree, fueling the especially high suicide rate among elderly white males. One man, for instance, following a despairing period of retirement years, left a suicide note about the proverbial straw that broke his camel's back: "I lost my hat today; after losing so much, that was one more loss than I could handle."[16]

But despite the hardships that can accompany retirement, there is one coping skill that is available to all and singularly powerful: planning. Commonly the workers who refuse to plan reason that they will not live long enough to retire, or they reason that they will stay busy the rest of their lives. And the workers who are most likely to resent having to retire are the highly educated, white-collar workers who have superior salary and job satisfaction. But regardless of pre-retirement criteria, case studies show that those who plan for retirement are far more likely to adjust successfully afterwards than those who did not plan.

But what issues should be included in preretirement planning? Sound planning will include *where to live, how to pay bills, how to maintain one's health,* and *which routine activities to include in one's lifestyle.*

And once retirement comes, there are likely to be three phases to this stage of life:

1. *The project phase*
    taking a trip
    fixing up the house
2. *The restless phase*
    looking for something to do
    adjusting to the retired role
3. *The stable phase*
    living with a new pattern of spending the day
    making friendships
    finding new activities
    living on a smaller budget

Most retirees adjust within three months and only 30 percent of them find little or nothing to enjoy about ongoing retirement.

One model for successful retirement is found in the biblical pattern of the Levites (Num. 8:23–26), allowing for the flexible reduction of work while maintaining an ongoing contribution to the group. The senior-sensitive church will encourage its elders to retire to something rather than simply retiring from something.

Look at Problems Creatively

If we are to age successfully, we will not only need to know God, to care for our bodies, to practice life-long learning, and to plan for retirement, we will need wisdom to approach our problems with creativity. To engage in creative problem solving, we will need to keep four principles in mind.

The first principle of creative problem solving during older adulthood is *to avoid tunnel vision by keeping an open perspective on problems.* Since adults are not guaranteed success or failure based simply on their age or the nature of their problem, the questions below help identify other variables that can influence problem solving outcomes.[17]

1. The situation: How do you see it?
   Was the problem anticipated?
   Did the problem come at a good or bad time?
   Was the problem within your control?
   Are there other problems in life right now?
   Are there any desirable aspects to the problem?
   How long does it seem the problem will last?
   Have you experienced something similar to this before?

2. The support: How do you see it?
   Can you get help from family, friends, or groups?
   Will this support be long-term or short-term?
3. The self: How do you see it?
   Are you optimistic?
   Do you have physical and psychological energy?
   Can you take a different view of the situation?
   Can you control your reactions?
   Can you take action when necessary?
   Are you knowledgeable about your finances and
      health?
   What really matters to you?
   Can you talk to someone who's been through
      this before?
   Can you relax?
   Can you build your strengths?

If you or someone you know is working through a problem, consider working through these probing questions
to keep your perspective open and to avoid tunnel
vision.

The second principle of creative problem solving during older adulthood is *to recognize that longevity is a
mixed blessing.* Though life expectancy in America has
nearly doubled over the last century—creating new
potentialities for the older adult years—medical science
has made nearly zero progress in resolving chronic
degenerative diseases; we merely prolong dying.

Furthermore with people living longer but retiring
earlier, the ratio of workers to retirees is quickly on its
way to dropping threefold, seriously jeopardizing the
Social Security system.

In addition national trends suggest that if we built a
120-bed nursing home daily throughout the decade of

the 1990s, America would still not have enough space for the 1 in 20 senior adults who will still need it by the turn of the century. And based on these demographics, the specter of socialized medicine looms on the horizon at least by the year 2030.

In sum we cannot decide that the sole goal in life is to live longer and longer, and that if achieved, this goal would cure all ills. Longevity is a hybrid of advantages and disadvantages. The wise person will see both sides realistically, surrendering both the fear of death and the idolization of life.

The third principle of creative problem solving during older adulthood is *to learn from the example of other vital adults.* To avoid tunnel vision and to make the most of our ambiguous longevity, we need to practice the qualities of pathfinders, people who have handled life's transitions particularly well. Such people, according to developmental data, are able to affirm the following qualities.[18]

My life has meaning and direction.

I have experienced one or more important transitions during my adult years in a positive way.

I rarely feel cheated or disappointed by life.

I have already attained several of the long-term goals that are important to me.

I am pleased with my personal growth and development.

I am in love; my partner and I love mutually.

I have many friends.

I am a cheerful person.

I am not thin-skinned or sensitive to criticism.

I have no major fears.

Although there is no path that is totally free of pain, we can learn from the sojourners who have gone before and seek to help those who are coming after us (Heb. 11:1–12:3; 1 Cor. 10:11–13).

The fourth principle of creative problem solving during older adulthood is *to reach out to others in need.* Our Lord, from the cross, reached out to the thieves, to his mother and John, and to the soldiers. Just as he reached out to us in our need, so he can give us strength to reach out to another person, even during our apparent weakness.

As we care for others we become like broken bread and crushed grapes—his life-giving brokenness. No wine ever quenched thirst until the grape was broken; no bread ever remedied hunger until the crust of the loaf was cracked. When our burdens seem as if they are going to bury us, we can trust God for his strength to reach out to another in need.

In reaching out to others some ministries are nearly always available: being a loving listener for somebody who is discouraged (James 1:19, 27), being a spiritual grandparent to a younger person (Gen. 48:1, 5, 8–20), and sensitizing people to the needs and competencies of older adults (1 Tim. 5:1–3, 8, 17–19).

In conclusion a God-pleasing life seeks to respond to the challenges of change. Even at age eighty-five Caleb was willing to conquer a new mountain in God's strength (Josh. 13:1; 14:6–15; 15:13–15). While the Hemlock Society fuels the rhetoric about the quality of life, God is enabling true pathfinders to discover eternal life (John 17:3). Though the world values how we look, what we own, and what we do, the God of the ages values who we are and who we can become in him (1 Sam. 16:7b; 2 Cor. 3:18).

Discussion Questions

1. Why might it have been difficult for Timothy to make the transition into being the primary caregiver to the aged apostle Paul?

2. Name three of the most striking metaphors in Psalm 90 about the frailty of man. What does the psalmist ask God for and what difference would those requests make, if granted?

3. Describe three aging-related physical changes you have observed in yourself or someone else. Role-play the declining elder by doing two of the following activities for four hours in your normal routine: put scotch tape on your eyeglasses (or wear yellow-tinted sunglasses), put wet cotton balls in your ears, wear gloves, tape a section of newspaper around your knees. (Be sure to take appropriate safety precautions.)

4. If you had no other knowledge than what you learned from television, what would you think it means to be old? How might this information affect you as you grew older?

5. How might you explain the Gallup findings that spirituality seems to generally increase with age? Do you think older adults are any less likely to be converted than younger adults?

6. Describe why it is important to accept new physical limitations and to maintain an optimistic outlook on life.

7. What are some differences between how younger people and older people learn?

8. If you were counseling an older adult, using the ideas of transcendence vs. preoccupation, how would you challenge them toward maximum living?

9. Name three guidelines in planning for retirement.

10. Why is longevity ambiguous?

8

The Mentoring of Children

As the helicopter roared skyward, the once-serene playground turned instantly into a dusty whirlwind. Where children had played duck-duck-goose, a tearful mother strained to watch her son's only hope shrink toward the sun.

Cory, now seven, had been battling cancer for two years. His little body had now become home for clusters of tumors, jagged scars, and treatment burns.

As the minitornado settled into an eerie calm, a tearful mother began sprinting toward her dented car to rush by godspeed to Children's Hospital. Every emotion throttled through her personality: "Will Cory make it alive? Has he died already on the Med-Evac chopper? If this is the end, I'm not ready for it!"

After what seemed like an eternity, the battle-weary mother stood amid a roomful of pulsating machinery. Like unblinking soldiers standing watch over a lifeless boy, the equipment stubbornly denied Cory permission to die. Unclothed but for a white washcloth at his middle, tubes and monitors connected him to life. "A stroke, massive hematoma pressing on the brain. They give him twenty-four hours to live," the maternal warrior whispered as husband, pastor, and grandparents successively arrived in stunned silence.

After weeks of insistent prayer, minimiracles, and the mysterious will to live, Cory could speak again. It wasn't his time to die—and he knew it. His ballgame was going into extra innings, and he was going into the medical books. He'd recover enough to ride a two-wheeler, always sporting Grandpa's hat. He'd forget most everything he knew but would begin again with his homemade classroom of learning. Make-A-Wish! would send him to Disney World and he'd make the papers. Not long afterward, Cory would find himself sitting with his nana, talking like a veteran about the realities of her new lymphoma.

Cory has trusted Christ since his original diagnosis and expects to sit a lot closer to Jesus than others in heaven due to his unusual sufferings. And when Cory's time does come, he's planning to become his mother's guardian angel until she joins him on heaven's ever-calm playground.

From courageous kids like Cory, we have learned something about the art of mentoring children, both sick children and well. And thus it is our decided purpose to teach and to model the principles for educating the young in the special truths of life and death.

Therapeutic Principles

Whether we are talking to a seasoned Med-Evac passenger like Cory or to his school chums, still playing duck-duck-goose, there are guiding principles for our well-intentioned therapy of words. The five death educational principles which follow are based on developmental theory, therapeutic communication, and age-appropriate pedagogy.

Work Within Developmental Norms

First of all sound death education with children must work within developmental norms, moving youngsters along at their own pace of readiness.[1]

Birth to Age 2	There is no concept of death. (These children experience absence but do not understand it.)
Ages 2–7	Death is temporary and reversible. (Death is like a departure or like sleep.)
Ages 7–12	Death is irreversible but not universal. (Death is final but not destined to touch everybody.)
Ages 12+	Death is universal. (Death is irreversible and personal, but usually distant.)

While the foregoing characteristics fit the typical child, atypical circumstances, like terminal illness or bereavement in the immediate family, have often crystallized the insight of children ahead of schedule.

Initiate Conversations Dealing with Death

Second, quality communication with adults maximizes a child's potential for grappling with life and death. Adults committed to this kind of ministry should use object lessons to describe the dying process and its consequences, comfortably using the word *dead* many times. Some readily available object lessons include the life cycle of a tree, the death of a pet, or television character, or public figure on the news.

Adults thoughtfully engaged in death education will also need to accept individual differences among children. These differences will influence how much the child can understand and wants to talk, as well as the child's particular ways of expressing feelings.

Furthermore supportive adults must be aware of the variety of potential grief responses in children, responses that include denial, guilt, anger, idealization, identification, replacement, bargaining, depression, and physical symptoms. A child's grief should only be considered pathological when it is significantly delayed, distorted, or prolonged.

Adults who speak the truth in love to children will model excellent interpersonal communication, using eye contact, physical touch, empathic listening, personal disclosure, concrete labeling, permission to question, and reassurance of the knowns. Adults using these qualities will not lie or use overly abstract explanations such as "he went on vacation, fell asleep, got sick and died, or went to heaven because God loved him so much."

The adults who do use deception, generalization, or abstraction will usually be protecting themselves, not the child. Such behaviors will harm the adult's credibility and sometimes sponsor unnecessary fears in the child.

Instead adults should use accurate explanations and assurances, suggesting disclosures like this: "Grandpa had a disease called cancer which the doctors can usually cure; it just didn't work this time. It wasn't anyone's fault. Most people don't get cancer so we don't have to worry about that. If Mommy or Daddy had it, we'd tell you. Parents don't usually die until their children are all grown up and have a family of their own; but if we did die while you were younger, you would go to live with Uncle Jerry and Auntie Lois."

Adults in key relationships with bereaved children will understand the importance of rites of passage for them. Wakes, funerals, and interments will help confront the death and signal the beginning of change.

But there are excellent alternatives to the formal rites when circumstances make this advisable—alternatives like farewell visits, bringing flowers to the grave, memory sessions, cleaning out belongings, viewing old pictures and gifts, and keeping a memento. In general children will want to be included with the family and have a sense of belonging.

When attending a formal rite, children should be told in advance what they will see and hear, with an adult accompanying them at all times. Calm, generous answers will be the order of the day for those adults who pair up with the various children.

A child who does not wish to attend a rite should not be forced to or shamed for their feelings. But assigning an alternative role, like helping a neighbor guard the house from robbery during the funeral, or preparing part of the mercy meal, can help the child fill the void left from nonparticipation in the public rite.

Use Transition Illustrations

Adults in dialogue with children will find it helpful to use death analogies which emphasize transition instead of cessation—analogies such as:

A caterpillar changing into a butterfly, leaving the chrysalis behind

Moving out of one house, leaving it empty, while moving into a new house (2 Cor. 5:1)

Collapsing a tent, leaving the empty tent behind and hiking on to a new campsite (2 Tim. 4:6)

Needing a passport to enter a new country, just as we need faith in Christ to enter heaven

Use Age-Appropriate Descriptions of Heaven

As adults describe heaven for children, they'll find that the concept of rest, generally appealing to the elderly, will be meaningful only to the weary, terminal child. Instead, heaven as a happy, beautiful, active place will seem more age-appropriate for typical children. But be careful not to exaggerate or sensationalize heaven as if it were some kind of escapist fantasy, an image that could add to the growing number of childhood suicides. A safe, biblical model would describe heaven as too wonderful for words (2 Cor. 12:4) and free of the earth's worst realities (Rev. 21:4, 25; 22:3).

Fortunately our death educational work with children can be significantly boosted by the numerous children's books which are now available. Some will be specialized to coach the adult mentor, while the rest are designed for direct use with children. Of the latter, of course, some will be Bible-based, while others will be naturalistic.

An Example of Mentoring Children

I am convinced that the best starting point for any death education curriculum is the Bible.[2] Furthermore if we are going to communicate the Bible effectively to young minds, there is no better technique than storytelling, especially if the stories emphasize action, utilize imagination, and permit flexible adult-child dialogue.

To model biblical storytelling for death education, we will recount the life of Paul, told as if the listeners were late elementary-age children. When doing this kind of storytelling, the visual impact can always be enhanced through the use of pictures, a map, a time line, or drama. But regardless of teaching style, the goal will always be to rehearse a model of life and death that is biblical, interesting, and interpersonally healthy.

Paul Growing Up[3]

"A boy!" Paul's mother smiled happily. "A new son!" nodded his proud father. Not only did Paul's birth excite his parents, it also sent his eight-year-old sister jumping up and down, almost nonstop. But somebody else was joyful that day too: God.

Up in heaven, the Lord had known exactly what Paul would look like, even while he was still inside his mother's body. In fact long before Paul was born, God had said, "He will grow up to serve me with bravery, traveling the world, and boldly telling others about me."

As little Paul grew up, his parents and his big sister told him lots of Bible stories. Paul loved these story-times and dreamed about being a strong leader like King Saul, or a brave warrior like Benjamin, or a missionary like Jonah.

Paul's father smiled most broadly whenever he talked about being a Roman citizen. "We belong to the strongest country in the world," he'd say, "and you should be proud to be part of it, son!" Paul always agreed and you could tell he meant it the way he cheered, watching parades of Roman soldiers with their flags and armor. *The best part is the Roman Games!* the young citizen thought. The big, Olympic-type sports contests always thrilled Paul, especially the boxing and the foot races.

Besides telling stories and watching the Roman Games, Paul's family also had fun camping together. Their favorite place to camp was outside of Tarsus, in a grassy field next to the Sparkling River. They enjoyed swimming or just lying in the soft meadow, watching the clouds dance by. In time Paul's family started making tents for sale in the market.

When Paul was in school, he worked very hard on his assignments, usually getting straight As. One day, his teacher announced: "Paul has studied so well that next year, when he turns thirteen, he can go to the best school in the nation!" Paul was going to be allowed to move to Jerusalem, live with his sister, and study to become a lawyer under Dr. Gamaliel. Dr. Gamaliel was going to teach him to understand all the laws of the Bible and how to solve problems when people couldn't get along. Paul was going to become a special assistant to the judges and policemen, helping decide who should go to jail and who should go free.

Paul couldn't believe his ears when the teacher made the announcement! This news was too good to be true! But Paul make one big mistake. He didn't thank God. In fact he did the opposite. Paul stuck out his chest and taunted, "I'm going to Gamaliel's school in Jerusalem because I am so smart and so perfect! I don't need anyone to help me with my life!"

The Stoning of Stephen[4]

"Squeak-bump, squeak-bump," the heavy, wooden wagon groaned toward Jerusalem. After celebrating his thirteenth birthday, Paul was finally on his way to the big city to live with his sister and her husband. As the horses slowed to a stop in front of Paul's new home, his mind was filled with questions: "What will it be like to study at Dr. Gamaliel's school? Will I still be able to get all As here? Will I become a famous lawyer someday?"

Over the next several years Paul's questions began to be answered and his dreams started to come true. He read hundreds of books, memorized all the laws in the Bible, and became the top student in Dr. Gamaliel's school. He even outscored the guys who were older than him in the city-wide contests, where the students used laws to give speeches and win arguments.

Probably two of the traits that helped Paul win his contests were his anger and his pride. Paul would picture the person he was up against as the enemy and he'd never admit he was wrong. He just kept pushing his point as hard as he could, even if he had to use cruel words to win. God hadn't changed Paul on the inside yet.

When Paul graduated from Dr. Gamaliel's school, he

started working for the leaders of the Jerusalem temple. These leaders, called "The Seventy," wanted lawyers like Paul to enforce the laws around Jerusalem. One thing they really liked about Paul was that he was proud and angry, just like them.

One day as Paul was walking through the market past the fruit and vegetable carts, he was startled by a loud burst of sudden shouting. "What's going on?" he muttered to himself. And then he saw it: a huge, angry crowd up ahead, pushing and screaming.

Hurrying over, Paul demanded an explanation: "What's happening here?" A tall man on the fringe of the crowd growled back his answer. "It's that Stephen! He's so crazy that he believes in Jesus! And he's been telling everybody else they have to obey him, too! On top of that, the fool's just gone too far! Just a few minutes ago, Stephen told The Seventy that they were wrong to kill Jesus and that God is going to judge them. 'Soon,' he said!"

In a furious rush the fellow threw his coat toward Paul, spitting out the command: "Hold this! I'll fix Stephen!" In an instant this guy was scooping up large rocks along the road. "Let's stone him!" several screamed at once. The crowd pushed Stephen up against a wall and stepped back. The first stone smashed above his eye sending bright-red blood like teardrops down his face. Stephen didn't even try to run or fight back as a small boulder was heaved, knocking him to his knees. Soon Paul's arms were filled with coats as he stared at the gang murder, unfolding before his eyes.

Stephen's body was in terrible pain, but his spirit was peaceful. The outside part of Stephen was being brutally killed, but the inside part was not confused or crying, was not fighting back, or calling his attackers names. The Lord had changed Stephen on the inside. Paul kept looking straight at Stephen, whispering, "Looks like a clear white light, shining on his face!"

Just then Stephen glanced up at the blue sky and the clouds slid back. It was as if Jesus had opened the curtains so Stephen could peek right in heaven's window. "There's Jesus and his arms are open, ready to hug me home," Stephen mouthed. "Lord Jesus, forgive these men for what they are doing," he said softly.

But the stones kept coming and soon Stephen's body fell down flat on the ground—dead. His body became quiet and still, empty and dead. As quick as you can blink your eye, Jesus sent kind, invisible angels to whisk Stephen's spirit to heaven so that he could be with Jesus and all the friends there. Stephen began his long hug, happy to be in a place where everyone loved him, a place where there would never be any darkness, sickness, or crying, a place where no one would ever be mean again.

All over Jerusalem, Stephen's friends were very sad; not sad because he was in heaven, but sad because they were going to miss him. Although they knew that heaven would be joyfully busy for Stephen, they were sorry about the angry mob, sorry that they wouldn't be able to see their friend for many years. As they picked up Stephen's body, the friends headed toward a house to clean and dress him, getting ready to bury the body in a grave.

For a long time afterward Paul kept standing there beside the bloody road, wondering. As the men who had hurled the stones took their coats from him, he kept asking himself: "Was Stephen a good man or a bad man?" Paul couldn't decide; he was puzzled by what he saw that day.

The Blinding Light[5]

Paul couldn't sleep that night, tossing and turning on his bed, questions whizzing through his mind. "Who was right? Stephen or the men who had killed him?" Every time Paul tried to close his eyes, his memory would repaint the picture of Stephen's beautiful but bloody face. "Maybe Stephen was a good man; he seemed so new and different on the inside!" Paul'd whisper madly as if talking to his pillow. Then shaking his head, he'd shout, "No! Stephen must have been wrong! How could he tell The Seventy that Jesus was God's Son? How could God's Son die on the cross? God can't die; that's impossible!"

By morning, Paul had made up his mind. "Stephen must have been wrong, just like Jesus was wrong!" he muttered. "Today I'm going straight to The Seventy to help them get rid of these crazy Christians. People like Stephen, who believe that Jesus is God's Son, are just confusing everybody, causing one problem after another!"

Pleased to hear that Paul was willing to help, The Seventy began giving instructions. "Take these temple soldiers so you can arrest anyone you find who believes as Stephen did. If you find some of those troublemakers, bring them back to Jerusalem and we'll lock them up in jail here."

Armed with his instructions, Paul and the soldiers took off, ready to work. House to house, they began knocking on doors. "Open up! Any Christians in there?" Those who had courage to answer, "Yes," were promptly handcuffed, slapped around, and marched off to jail.

Within a few weeks, The Seventy sent Paul on a journey to a faraway city. "Go to Damascus," they said, "and arrest the Christians there!" But as Paul and his soldiers began marching up the dusty road toward Damascus, a surprising thing happened. *Flash*, a bright lightning filled the sky. *Boom*, thundered the deafening noise. Knocked to the ground by the flash and the boom, Paul tried to look around. "I can't see!" he screamed. "It's not dirt in my eyes; everything is darkness—I'm blind!"

Suddenly Jesus' booming voice from the sky spoke: "Why are you attacking me?" Paul stared up into the darkness. "Who are you?" he asked weakly. As Paul listened for an answer, he noticed his body was shaking with fear. "I am Jesus," the voice thundered, "the One you are attacking. Stop arresting and hurting the people who love me."

Right then Paul realized that Jesus was God's Son. Jesus was alive, talking to him on the Damascus Road. Paul began to pray slowly, "Lord Jesus, I'm sorry for all the wrong things I've said and done. Now I know you died on the cross to help me, to make me new on the inside like Stephen. Thank you for loving me and please help me to obey you from now on."

As Paul lay there, his tears of joy began to drip on the dusty road. In the stillness something else began to happen, too: God began sending new friends to Paul. One friend, Ananias, came and healed Paul's blind eyes. Other friends took him to their home and taught him more about the Bible and how to be a missionary. One of them, Barnabas, brought Paul to church and showed the Christians that Paul wasn't playing a trick. He really was changed on the inside.

But not everybody was happy with Paul, now that he was changed on the inside. The Seventy in Jerusalem were furious. "Paul's our enemy now," they raged. "We need to kill him just like we killed Stephen!"

Pretty soon new soldiers began arriving in Damascus with orders to kill Paul. One night, after the city gates closed, these soldiers began going house to house to find Paul. "We'll kill him by morning," they bitterly promised. As the soldiers neared Barnabas's house, Paul's friend warned, "They're just down the street. We've got to do something! Quick! Here, climb in this large basket. We'll let you down by rope through that window in the city wall." Just moments before the soldiers knocked on Barnabas's door, Paul's basket touched down outside the wall. Running away in the moonlight, Paul found a ship to sail him away from the evil soldiers. Climbing aboard the ship, he silently promised, *Lord Jesus, even if it is dangerous, I will obey you and keep telling people about you.*

Missionary Journeys [6]

Since Paul and Barnabas had become best friends, everyone was pleased when the Lord asked them to become a missionary team. Gladly obeying, they took along Barnabas's teenage cousin, John Mark, and sailed away on a ship to find people in other lands who hadn't heard about Jesus.

But once they were ashore, Paul couldn't convince John Mark not to be afraid of the strangers they were meeting on their first island. In fact one morning, long before Paul and Barnabas were awake, John Mark ran away. Hurrying to the harbor, he jumped on a ship and sailed back home. This bothered the older men, but they continued hiking from village to village on the island, telling people about Jesus. Then, after three years of hard work like this, Paul and Barnabas returned home for a rest.

After their rest, Paul and Barnabas each started their own team of missionaries, Aquila and Priscilla joining in with Paul. Paul had a great plan: his team would make tents during the day to earn food money and then teach Bible classes about Jesus in the evening.

The plan worked all right for several months until something backfired. Late one afternoon, Paul took some of the tents down to the market and sold them just before dinner. While the crowd was still gathered around, he climbed up on a box and began telling the story of Jesus. All of a sudden, Whack! A big soldier sent Paul tumbling off his box, swinging his spear like it was a baseball bat. "You're under arrest. These people don't want to hear about Jesus. You're going to the lions, right now!" the gladiator raged.

Hurrying Paul off to the stadium, this burly soldier threw him out into the ring of lions with an evil laugh. At the other end of the oval field, the lions began sniffing at the air, ready for dinner.

Aquila and Priscilla, out of breath from trying to keep up with the soldier, arrived at the stadium a few minutes later. Shouting out last minute instructions, Priscilla barked, "I'll pray; you go to the Governor of the Games and beg for mercy on Paul."

Aquila, leaping up the stadium steps two at a time, quickly found the governor and blurted: "Sir, please rescue our friend, Paul. He's a Roman citizen and he hasn't hurt anyone!" Before the surprised governor could answer, the lions roared to begin their attack! Turning anxiously, Aquila saw one lioness swing her knifelike paw, gashing Paul's shirt, turning it into a wet red.

Looking into Aquila's eyes, the Governor spit out his decision: "Okay, I'll help." Without breaking eye contact, the governor continued, "Lieutenant, send a rider!" Receiving his signal with the sword, a horseman galloped out onto the field, swooping Paul up with one strong arm.

Once safely outside the stadium fence, Paul slid down from the horse, gazing at his bloody chest. As Paul sunk to the ground, his friends began tightly wrapping cloth around his wounds. "Thank you for being so brave," Paul whispered. "The governor could have sent you out into the ring for arguing with him." Without a word, Aquila just hugged Paul's neck, "Thank God, not me."

Even though missionary life had proven dangerous that day, Paul and his team continued doing their work for the Lord. And just as there were danger days, as when Paul was thrown to the lions, there were also miracle days, days of friendship when God did mighty things for them. In time Paul, Aquila, and Priscilla boarded their ship, bidding farewell to their new friends, and sailing toward home.

Arrested and Shipwrecked [7]

The morning after Paul was back in Jerusalem, he invited his friends to join him for worship in the temple. So dressed in their brightest clothes, the three of them walked briskly toward the temple. Entering through the golden doors, everyone became quiet, hushed as the crowd listened to the music and smelled the candles.

Grateful to be home again, Paul closed his eyes to pray. But before he could even whisper a word, the stranger next to him shoved him hard, sprawling him to the floor. "Who are you?" the man growled at Paul. "You don't belong here. I can tell from your clothes and your haircut that you are from another country!"

Soon more people were shouting. "Get out, you dirty dogs! You're ruining our temple!" Before Paul could even answer, the crowd began pushing closer. Angry words whistled past Paul's ears. As if he were in the middle of a cyclone, the mob circled closer, threatening with their fists. *What's going to happen?* Paul thought. *Will I be killed like Stephen?*

Just then, a strong hand grabbed tightly onto Paul's wrist. A Roman soldier! One, two, three—a whole group of them, rescuing Paul from the wild crowd! Paul tried explaining as the soldiers rushed him through the crowd, out of the temple. "We don't care about your excuses," they shot back. "You're under arrest for starting that fight back there!" "But I . . ." Paul tried to explain, uselessly; no one was listening.

With Paul in jail, the officers began arguing about what to do with him. Some people wanted him killed; others wanted him set free. But since he was a Roman citizen, they chained him to a Roman soldier named Pudens and boarded him on a prisoner ship bound for trial in Rome.

By sunrise Paul's ship was so far out to sea that Pudens unlocked his chains. Standing on the deck in the warm sun, Paul began to remember. "I knew Jesus told me I'd be a messenger to the leaders in Rome. But I never thought it would happen this way!" As the breeze filled the sails, Paul's ship cut through the water, day after day, week after week.

One night, while most of the passengers were sleeping, a fierce storm came up. The rain pelted the crew like bullets and the howling fury drove the ship farther off course in the darkness. The old wooden ship began to creak and groan like it was going to shatter from the next wave. Paul began praying as the captain shouted, "This is it! This ship's not going to make it. Prepare to crash; everyone's going to drown."

Paul climbed out onto the deck and cupped his hands to speak above the howling wind. "The Lord says we must throw all of our luggage into the sea. After we crash, we are to swim with a broken board till daylight. By morning we'll find land and no one will drown; it's not time for us to die."

Soon the ship splintered apart, dumping everyone into the dark waters. Grabbing a large plank and steering it toward three others coughing nearby, Paul hung on in exhaustion, wondering about Pudens.

By morning light each of the passengers had spotted a small island. Using their planks like wooden rafts, they kicked themselves toward shore. Once Paul was on dry land, he caught his breath and began pulling others up onto the sand. "Where's Pudens?" he kept muttering under his breath, "Where's Pudens?"

There in the distance, Paul spotted the soldier pulling himself out of the water. Hurrying to his companion, Paul blurted out the question which had haunted him through the long hours of the stormy night. "Pudens, if you had drowned last night in the water, what would have happened?" The soldier looked puzzled. "If the Lord hadn't protected you and your outside body had died, would your inside spirit have gone to heaven?" The wet guard sat down on the beach and just shook his head, confused.

Pudens shot back his own questions as if hungry for an answer, "How can I know for sure if I would go to heaven when I die?" Paul began, "You know what a passport is, don't you? It's that special piece of paper you need to travel from one country to another. If you don't have it, you can't enter." Paul paused as Pudens leaned closer. "When our body dies," Paul continued, "our spirit travels. As fast as you can blink your eye, you can travel to God's country, heaven; but only if you have a passport!" Pudens' eyes brightened up, "A passport for heaven?" "Yes," Paul smiled, "but it's not something you can buy or make. The passport for entering heaven is believing in Jesus. If people ask the Lord to forgive them for the wrong things they've done, to make them new on the inside, that's the passport. That lets you enter heaven when you die. And once you have it, you can never lose it."

Pudens had a lot of questions but Paul patiently answered each one. Before long the strong soldier knelt on the beach and prayerfully thanked Jesus for dying on the cross. Now he had his own passport for heaven.

In a few days a new ship came and everyone got on board to finish the trip to Rome. But unlike the rest of the passengers Paul was actually joyful that God had sent the storm and the shipwreck. The disaster at sea had let Paul be a missionary to the Roman soldier and had helped Pudens get the passport for heaven.

When Paul arrived in Rome, he was hoping that his problem would be solved quickly—but it wasn't. The Roman judges wrote a letter and asked The Seventy to send someone from Jerusalem to explain why Paul had been arrested. Day after day, week after week, month after month, The Seventy didn't respond. While Paul was waiting in jail, he wrote letters to the churches, received visits from friends, and continued to be a missionary to the Roman soldiers.

Then, after two years of waiting, the judges released Paul. "You're a Roman citizen," they said. "And if your accusers are not going to send criminal charges against you, you're free. Just stay out of trouble." Off came the chains and the wooden cell door creaked open. Blinking in the sunlight, Paul stared as the food wagons passed him by on the dusty Roman streets. Stumbling over to the water fountain, Paul washed his face and took a deep drink.

Before long Paul was traveling as a missionary again. After visiting some of the places he had been before, he went as far west as Spain telling more people about Jesus.

Many years later, when Paul was about sixty, the wicked King Nero arrested him. While waiting in jail for Nero's decision, Paul wrote this letter to his younger friend, Timothy. (See 2 Tim. 4.)

Dear Timothy,

I have gotten older now and my body is weaker. Would you please visit me in the jail and bring me my coat? I get cold very easily now. Would you also bring me my books? I forget things more often than I used to. I feel the time is coming soon when I will die. When King Nero kills my body, my spirit will go to heaven. My body will be like an empty hollow tent after I am dead, buried like an empty, old tent is folded up and put away. But the real me, my inside spirit, will go to heaven. I will be with Jesus and Stephen and all of the other friends who died with the passport to heaven.

I feel like I have been in school, having learned so much in life. I feel like I have been in a long race, too, ready to cross the finish line, like I've been in a big fight and won. When I get to heaven, the Lord is going to give me a crown. A shiny, beautiful crown called the "Crown of Life." This crown will be mine because Christ is kind, because I have lived life his way, and because he changed me with his new life on the inside.

Your friend,
PAUL

Shortly after the apostle wrote this letter, King Nero chopped off Paul's head. Immediately he arrived in heaven to stay forever.

Create a Vision of Heaven

Many people who think about death today would reject the biblical story of Paul as a mere fairy tale. They might question how he or Stephen could claim to have peace in the face of death, how he could honestly picture himself being welcomed by Jesus into heaven.

This same skepticism paralyzed Dr. Diane Komp the first time she sat at the bedside of a dying child.[8] Committed to sharing the final hours of life with her seven-year-old leukemia patient, this agnostic pediatrician was at the dreaded bedside out of sober duty. With her religious convictions completely derailed since medical school, this doctor anticipated no joy in the events that were about to unfold. But to her confused delight, Komp witnessed the sudden infusion of energy into the little patient's body. The dying girl sat straight up in her final moments with words of pure thrill: "The angels, they're so beautiful! Mommy, can you see them? Do you hear their singing? I've never heard such beautiful singing."

From this little girl and many like her since, Dr. Komp has learned the secret of life beyond the grave. Christian children with visions of heaven reflect a peace which passes even medical understanding.

Discussion Questions

1. How might you be feeling if you were the mother of seven-year-old Cory, watching the Med-Evac helicopter lift off? If you were Cory?
2. Imagine you are a child whose grandfather just died of a sudden heart attack. How might you understand his death if you were a three-year-old? Five? Nine? Fourteen? Imagine you are a child with terminal leukemia; how might you understand your coming death if you were a three-year-old? Five? Nine? Fourteen?
3. Find one object lesson in the next twenty-four hours that you could use to teach a child something about aging, grief, or death.

4. Identify one of the potential grief responses of children that seems most like your style of grieving. Describe the most unhealthy grief response you've ever witnessed.

5. Describe an occasion where you recall an adult using deception, generalization, or abstraction to answer a child's question about death.

6. What would you do if someone said to you: "My wife just died and our eight-year-old does not want to go to the funeral"?

7. Compare one death educational book for children that is Bible-based with another that is naturalistic.

8. Choose a biblical story and develop a death-educational strategy for telling that story.

9. How did you react to the child's deathbed vision of angels?

9

The Care of Sufferers

Sue's mind raced excitedly as she lay in the delivery room, her mind flashing pictures of Steve, throwing the football and picking huckleberries with their new son, Matthew.[1]

What's Wrong with Matthew?

But Steve and Sue's exhilaration was immediately tested as Matthew, weighing less than three pounds, was whisked away to an incubator. Born premature with cerebral palsy, Matthew would struggle eventually to lift his head, roll over, and speak his first word, "Mama." Tragically, it would be his only word. Part of the medical miracle that had kept Matthew alive in the early days were twenty tiny transfusions, each only a few teaspoons of blood. But, as the family would later learn, three of these minute transfusions had come from an AIDS carrier, keeping Matthew from ever reaching twenty pounds in his infection-filled body.

At first the doctors were baffled. Painful tests seemed to rule out every logical option until one day a physician gave them his hunch: AIDS. Gratefully relieved that a diagnosis had been reached and devouring every bit of ground-breaking information available, Matthew's parents refused to believe all was lost.

Since there was no family history of homosexuality, IV drug use, or connections to Haiti, the hospital team concluded that Matthew's transfusions had written his obituary. As pressure mounted to locate the infected donors, another baby died from the same transfusions.

While the Kozups pushed for early identification and full disclosure with the American Red Cross, they stubbornly camouflaged their ordeal in private. Feeding Matthew through a tube and changing his diaper with rubber gloves, Steve and Sue were unable to kiss their son or allow his sister to share his toys. Rejected from special education groups, the Kozups refused to tell their friends of Matthew's true condition.

In time an angelic nurse emerged as Matthew's hospital mom, eliciting smiles when everyone else was met by frightened cries. But Matthew still found a measure of joy in living: watching people, shredding napkins, and studying the sway of treetops in the wind, ways to keep a tiny boy distractedly busy.

As Matthew's coughing fits worsened, morphine couldn't stop the pain. On his three-and-a-half-year birthday, a little lad who had never walked, spoken a sentence, or played with other children, died. With his father's hand gently across his tiny back, his last torturous rattle was expelled. Sixteen pounds of loving silence lay still in the bed.

Steve and Sue felt like they were wearing lead weights as they made funeral arrangements, choosing a cemetery plot in the shade of a tree like Matthew would've liked, buying a new blue sleeper for his resting wardrobe. On the morning of Matthew's funeral, the grieving family was awakened by the noise and sight of their garbage truck crushing Matthew's crib, the AIDS crib that Sue couldn't give away.

Now, Steve visits the cemetery every day, somehow sensing that his little boy is unprotected there without him. Even during the night, these grieving parents hear Matthew's cry and jump to their feet, awakening en route to their solemn reality. And resting on Matthew's grave is a wooden heart, carved from a piece of firewood, now cracked down the middle by a blizzard.

Little Matthew's story touches on three critical dimensions in suffering: *initial impacts, sustained responses,* and *mature caregiving.* In suffering it is common for acute pain, like the Kozups had, to engender a wide variety of opening feelings. But despite the drama of the early stages, some ongoing coping styles usually emerge and are sustained over time. Furthermore the suffering creates potential for refining mature love, as it did for Matthew's parents and nurse. Since these dimensions are present in every experience of acute or chronic suffering, they form the organizing framework for this chapter.

The Cry of Sufferers: Initial Impacts

When we suffer, our first instinct is to ask: "Why? Why me? Why now? Why this?" This question comes first and lasts longest.[2] And this very quest for meaning led the grief poet to open three laments with the penetrating probe, "How?" (Lam. 1:1; 2:1; 4:1).

Job, the Classic Sufferer

The classic sufferer in the Bible, Job, serves as a model for exploring the meaning of suffering. While many sufferers identify with Job's experiences, no one can honestly derive a single-orbed theology from his book. In fact, the inspired potpourri of ideas throughout the book allows the reader to look at suffering like white light coming through a prism. All of the different colors, all of the different meanings for suffering, are present in the whole white light.

> Suffering is punishment for sin (Job 4:7).
> Suffering is a natural part of life (5:7).
> Suffering is for personal growth (42:1–6).
> Suffering is for public example (1:8; 42:10).

The Complexity of Suffering

While the variety of ideas in the Book of Job does not suggest that suffering is beyond reason, it does suggest that suffering is multifaceted, thus warning us against oversimplifying the meaning of anyone's suffering.

And since the four themes on the meaning of suffering could be easily correlated to other biblical incidents and modern-life experiences, counselors must discipline themselves not to be reductionistic in their therapeutic role. Imagine, for instance, if Jesus had come for help in understanding his crucifixion, how distorted the counseling might be if the helper had a narrow view of suffering. As is true in most suffering, Jesus' hardships merit a flexible combination of the themes, not a mutually exclusive, pigeonholing of "the cause." To illustrate, his death was a result of his natural humanity (Gen. 3:15; Heb. 2:9), served as punishment for sin (John 1:29; 2 Cor. 5:21), created the ultimate example (1 Peter 2:21), and sponsored his own personal growth (Heb. 5:7–9).

In an effort to honor the complexity of the sufferer's life, counselors can follow these principles.

Be a companion to sufferers.

Listen for statements of meaning from sufferers.

Analyze the sufferer's view of self, God, and others.

Invite the sufferer's global interpretation of life.

Validate the sufferer's perspective when it is therapeutic.

Reframe the sufferer's perspective when it is destructive.

In addition to building a therapeutic repertoire for helping the sufferer, the minister must also personally grapple with biblical priorities in God's design for suffering. While the five subsets of suffering listed below are all theologically important, the last category towers above the others in pastoral practice.

Ontology: "Does evil have an independent existence?"

Cosmology: "Where did evil come from?"

Taxonomy: "What kinds of suffering exist in the world?"

Axiology: "What kinds of values govern our responses to suffering?"

Teleology: "What kinds of ends might suffering be working out?"

This final question seems to have the direct attention of the Bible, being rooted in the heart of God. The Lord, it seems, is far more concerned with what is happening *in* the sufferer than what is happening *to* the sufferer. Thus God uses this priority of purpose to encourage the victims of an evil Nebuchadnezzar (Jer. 29:11–14). Likewise, Paul captures the teleology of increasing Christlikeness (Rom. 8:18, 24, 28–30).

Coping Mechanisms Used by Sufferers

The Bible clearly focuses on how we cope with suffering and what effect suffering is having upon us. In its realism we understand that there are no simple solutions, no heavenly escape routes, no quick fixes for the problems of pain. In Psalm 88 an honest sufferer refuses to minimize his pain or to exaggerate God's promises. Instead he composes the saddest psalm of the Bible, a grief lament which could well be called a miniature Job, perhaps sung while moving in a circle around the bed of a dying person.[3]

The Double ABCX Model

To analyze the suffering in Psalm 88, we will use the Double ABCX stress management model (Chart 3) which poses a hypothetical equation.

The A Factor: What were his circumstances? This grieving minstrel is terminally ill, suffering from a prolonged degenerative disease (Ps. 88:3, 15). Convinced that death is imminent, he sees his bedroom quickly becoming a tomb. Feeling as if he were dead already, the young man guesses that he's been moved from the town's register to the census of the deceased (v. 4). In painful metaphor, he sees himself lying on the bottom of the darkest ocean, buried far away from life (v. 6).

The B Factor: What was his support system? This pain-ridden patient has been abandoned by his family and friends who consider him repulsive (vv. 8, 18). Some of these loved ones may be superstitious, fearing he's contagious. Others just can't take his raw honesty, deciding instead to stay away. Although many potential caretakers have moved to the perimeter of this man's life, there had been one genuine friend, a fellow victim of the same ailment, now dead (v. 18). Without human sup-

Chart 3: The Double ABCX Stress Management Model[4]
A + B + C = X The *A* Factor = Stressor The *B* Factor = Coping Repertoire The *C* Factor = Definition of Stressor The *X* Factor = Crisis Impact The Double Factor = Previously Unresolved Stressors Piling Up

port, the psalmist attempts to draw strength from God, praying day and night for healing (vv. 1, 9, 13). But, it seems, God in his silence has rejected him (v. 14).

The C Factor: What was his personal outlook? Under such an avalanche of trouble, this sufferer acknowledges God as his only hope (vv. 1, 9, 13), struggling to prevent the rope of faith from slipping through his weary hands. Like Job this wounded warrior finds some measure of comfort in open, intense monologue with God. If he didn't believe that God existed, he wouldn't pray; if he didn't believe that God could heal, he wouldn't pour out his heart. And in the maelstrom of petition, this sufferer doesn't offer trite, controlled, little prayers. Instead, he pours out his confused, angry thoughts as Job did.

Fortunately, God understands that the pendulum of emotions is part of the coping process, not a theologically finished product. The energized thoughts are a part of seeking after truth yet to be revealed, not a blasphemous rebellion against truth already revealed.

And there is every confidence that God heard this prayer uttered from these depths as he heard Jonah's prayer from his. This psalmist does not promote a sick denial of what is happening—a panicky minimization of pain. Instead he faces the despairing reality and looks to hope beyond the circumstances, not hope in prayer, but hope in the God of prayer.

Caring for Sufferers

If we are going to effectively care for sufferers, we will need to understand our role as caregivers, offering mature love within a biblical framework for healing.

In our day, clergy have been commissioned to care for the sick in a spiritually wholesome way. But sadly some ministers anxiously avoid all reminders of their own mortality by abandoning the sick, hiding behind a rigid role, bickering over sheep stealing while parishioners lie in the hospital, and arguing the pragmatics of reaching youth instead of elders. Such pastoral buffoonery runs counter to the caring instincts of the Good Shepherd.

Effective Caregiving

An effective ministry to sufferers will be a discipline in balance.

Apathy ——— Empathy ———Sympathy

While the left end of the continuum is characterized by a lack of caring, the right end is known for its hypervigilance and enmeshment. Didn't Jesus censure the role of the apathetic priest and Levite as they passed by the wounded man on the Jericho Road (Luke 10:25–37)? Didn't he also chide the hyper-responsible Martha (vv. 38–42) who in this case might have been tempted to carry the wounded man on her back, rigidly foregoing her own needs out of sympathy for his pain?

In consummate balance the Good Samaritan modeled caring, without an obsession for quick-fix curing. Perhaps like Mary, the Good Samaritan ministered empathetically, as a person called by God, not driven by the panic of need. Thus he sacrificed some time, cleansed some wounds, shared his donkey, and hired an innkeeper for hospitality.

Likewise Paul challenged the Ephesians to practice an interpersonal spirituality, skillfully blending truth and love (Eph. 4:15), thus avoiding the brutality of truth alone or the sentimentality of love without limits. Such a pastoral outlook on people's multidimensional needs allows us to offer even a cup of cold water as a part of genuine caregiving (Matt. 25:34–36). When ministering with this kind of spiritual simplicity, we will, like the circus clown, use our creativity to help people, not so much by our expertise but by our humanity.[5]

Healing

For Today? When we care for sufferers, we inevitably encounter the question of healing. Hurting people crave to be free of pain, begging that doctors, ministers, or even God send them relief from their agony. Some, quite insistently, tell of promises made about imminent recovery, angrily naming those whose lies, once believed, have blossomed into disillusionment, sometimes indicting God himself.

If we are going to minister the Word of God and care for human sufferers, we will need to be ready for the question of healing. In particular, we will need to understand James 5:13–20, the most often quoted and most severely misunderstood text on divine healing.

In the Book of James. James challenges his readers to demonstrate genuine faith, waiting patiently for the Lord to return because judgment is coming on unbelievers (5:1–6), because the Lord is coming for his children (vv. 7–12), and because Elijah-type prayer can restore health (vv. 13–20). By blending the themes of patience, illness, and prayer, the Lord's half-brother teaches the importance of patience during illness and the source of patience in prayer. He furthermore encourages his readers through the example of Elijah (5:17–18) to trust God for any healing needed, body, soul, or spirit (vv. 13–16, 19–20).

With all of the misinformation about divine healing, it is imperative to state at the outset what James is *not* saying.

James 5:13–20 is not teaching . . .

There is a magical power or person.
   (The healing is "in the name of the Lord . . . who raises up.")
There is a magical place.
   (The sick person calls church elders to the bedside.)
There is a magical practice.
   (The elders use simple olive oil.[6])
There is an automatic connection between sin and illness.
   (James says: "If he has sinned . . .")
There is an automatic connection between prayer and healing.
   (James raises the possibility: "that you might be healed.")
Extreme unction
   (Healing, not death, is in view.)
Priestly absolution
   (The laity prays and mutually confesses sin.)
Works salvation
   (The wanderer, not the converter, is saved from sin.)

James exhorts his readers to patience, not only because judgment is coming on unbelievers (5:1–6) and because the Lord is coming for his children (vv. 7–12), but also because Elijah-type prayer can reverse illness and restore health (vv. 13–20). In the epilogue of his epistle, James exposes our need for patience in the face of illness, whether the illness be physical, psychosocial, or spiritual.

"Is any one of you in trouble? Pray," James advises (5:13). Instead of grumbling and swearing (vv. 9, 12), we should follow the example of the prophets (vv. 10–11), petitioning God for relief and filling our mouths with song.

"Is any one of you sick? Call," James counsels (vv. 14–15a), soliciting help from key caregivers. The elders are to pray for recovery, while daubing an all-purpose olive oil on the wounded region of the petitioner's body. With the historic example of elders serving primitive congregations like old-time country doctors, we are challenged to see the richest combination of spiritual and medical resources available.

Without idolizing the craft of modern medicine, or spiritualizing all medicine as the quackery of the world, we are grateful for our God-given abilities to increasingly harness nature for the common good. And with such a holistic interplay in view, one researcher has discovered that surgical patients, with the benefit of a personal companion, physical touch, and prayer in the pre-op area, require only half as much anesthesia to go to sleep, resting in the hands of the medical team and the everlasting arms of God.[7]

The crux of James's doctrine of healing comes in his definite promise: ". . . the prayer offered in faith will make the sick person well" (*see* 5:15). However, those interpreting this promise have understood it in three distinct ways.

A unique sickness (a sin-based illness)
A unique faith (an expectation of the supernatural)
A unique praying (with Elijah-like constancy)

In support of the first view, sin is mentioned four times in the context (vv. 15–16, 20), suggesting that a person could be inflicted with an illness from God in order to motivate repentance. The weakened person, once humbled by God through the illness, would begin healing on summons of the spiritual authorities and renewal of earnest, penitential prayer. Such a healing would be akin to Jesus healing the palsied man of both physical and spiritual illness at the same time (Mark 2:1–12), a scenario realistic to pastoral experience but not necessarily common.

The second option, a unique faith, can only be argued from New Testament examples like the woman with the blood disorder and Jairus's daughter, both of whom were healed because of special faith (Mark 5:22–23, 34, 36, 42). This kind of faith that moves mountains (Matt. 21:21–22) might be sourced in the sick person, the elders, or the congregation. But while this alternative is theologically possible, it is quite removed from the context of James 5.

The final interpretation suggests that unique praying, like that done by the widow (Luke 18:1–8) and by Elijah (James 5:16b–18), finds unusual responsiveness in God. This view is supported by a literal translation of James 5:16b: "A righteous person's petition avails a great deal when putting forth its energy."[8] This last option is more likely James's intent since he explicitly cites Elijah's constancy in prayer.

Though much has changed since James's day, our care of sufferers remains timelessly relevant. Though few of us now carry olive oil on visitation, we still hear the cry of sufferers, newly hurt, even if the cry first comes to us via answering machines. As ever, shepherdly men and women still monitor the ongoing walk of heaven's hurting lambs, coaching them to cope through the Good Shepherd.

And if we would be those whose life and work is sourced in the Chief Shepherd (1 Peter 5:4), we must be ever attuned to his voice, longing to see his truths about aging, grief, and death, focused through the lens of the Old and New Testaments. And when we see one of our sheep wince from the fear of death or the grief of loss, when we note a lamb limping from the wounds of suicide or suffering, we won't take an apathetic detour to the other side of the Jericho Road. For the whole flock, young or old, sick or well, we will respond with the courage to care in the power of Christ.

Discussion Questions

1. Compare how different people responded to Matthew Kozup's illness. Why do you think they responded as they did?
2. How do you feel about a sufferer who is asking, "Why?" About a sufferer who never asks, "Why?"
3. Of the themes on suffering in Job, which ones occur most instinctively to you?
4. Using the Double ABCX model, explain why two people can go through almost identical suffering but come out with nearly opposite impacts.
5. Describe a time when you were hurting and someone made hurtful remarks to you.
6. Are you more inclined toward apathy or sympathy in caregiving?

7. Do you see any parallel between the role of a clown and the role of a spiritual caregiver?
8. How do you feel about the healing movement in general?
9. How would you respond if a terminally ill patient asked you to pray for healing?

Notes

Preface

1. This monograph examines aging, grief, and death in the ancient Near East, the intertestamental period, the ancient and medieval church, and in modern religion. This supplement can be easily synthesized with the chapters of Part 1 to give historical continuity for researchers and teachers. The monograph is available at cost ($12.00 including postage and handling). Write to the author at 2909 Blueberry Lane, Bowie, MD 20715.

Part 1: Biblical Caregiving

1. Nigel Davies, *Human Sacrifice in History and Today* (New York: William Morrow, 1981), pp. 28–31.

Chapter 1: Why Should We Face Aging, Grief, and Death?

1. Robert C. Tate, Jr., "The Identification of Emotional Stress and Spiritual Needs of Senior Citizens in an Institutionalized Setting" (Ann Arbor, Mich.: Xerox University Microfilms, 1976), pp. 111–13.

2. Jeffrey A. Watson, *Looking Beyond—A Christian View of Suffering and Death* (Wheaton, Ill.: Victor, 1986), pp. 111–18.

3. Hannelore Wass and Charles A. Corr, *Helping Children Cope With Death* (New York: Hemisphere, 1984),pp. 2–3.

4. Robert Fulton, *Death, Grief, and Bereavement II* (New York: Arno Press, 1981), p. i.

5. The Listing Committee, *A Report: The 1981 White House Conference on Aging* (Washington, D.C.: Government Printing Office, 1981), pp. 82–204.

6. Jeffrey A. Watson, "The Flower Fadeth: A Pastoral Care Curriculum for Biblical Death Education in the Church," Brian P. O'Connor, ed. *The Pastoral Role in Caring for the Dying and the Bereaved* (New York: Praeger, 1986), pp. 31–40, 51–53.

7. M. E. Linn, B. S. Linn, and S. Stein, "Impact on Nursing Home Staff of Training about Death and Dying," *Journal of the American Medical Association* 250:17 (1983): 2332–35.

8. Robert M. Gray and David O. Moberg, *The Church and the Older Person* (Grand Rapids: Eerdmans, 1962), p. 91.

Chapter 2: How the Old Testament Helps Us Face Aging, Grief, and Death

1. Hugh Edwards, "Crocodile Attack" in *Reader's Digest* (October, 1989), pp. 70–75. Condensed from the book by the same author and title (New York: Harper & Row).

2. Roland de Vaux, *Ancient Israel* (New York: McGraw-Hill, 1965), 1:56.

3. Umberto Cassuto, *A Commentary on the Book of Genesis* (Jerusalem: Magnes Press, 1944), pp. 172–73.

Chapter 3: How the New Testament Helps Us Face Aging, Grief, and Death

1. Other Christians (amillennialists and postmillennialists) hold a different view of end-time events.

2. Joachim Jeremias, "Gehenna" in *Theological Dictionary of the New Testament* (Grand Rapids: Eerdmans, 1964) 1:656–57.

Part 2: Personal Caregiving

1. David Dempsey, *The Way We Die: An Investigation of Death and Dying in America Today* (New York: McGraw-Hill, 1975), pp. 26–27.

Chapter 4: The Fear of Death

1. Donald I. Templer, "The Construction and Validation of a Death Anxiety Scale," in *Journal of General Psychology*, 82 (1970), pp. 165–177.

2. Richard Lonetto and Donald I. Templer, *Death Anxiety* (Washington, D.C.: Hemisphere, 1986), pp. 4, 43, 56.

3. A true story with insignificant biographical details changed for confidentiality.

4. Jeff Collins, "Mother, Does It Hurt To Die?" in *Love and Action UPDATE* (Annapolis, Summer 1990), pp. 1–2.

5. Lonetto and Templer, *Death Anxiety*, pp. 7–37.

6. Ibid.

7. Evan McLeod Wylie, "Night Air Raid on Boston" in *Yankee Magazine* (Spring, 1990), pp. 78–81, 120–21.

8. "A Mighty Fortress" by Martin Luther, translated by Frederick H. Hedge.

Chapter 5: The Grief of Loss

1. A true story with insignificant biographical details changed for confidentiality.

2. Howard Clinebell, "The Five Tasks of Grief Work," a videotape in the series *Growing Through Grief—Personal Healing* (Claremont, Calif.: United Methodist Communications/Interfaith Media Center, 1974).

3. Patricia Weenolsen, *Transcendence of Loss Over the Life Span* (Washington, D.C.: Hemisphere, 1988), p. xi.

4. Ibid. pp. 20–23.

5. Bernice Neugarten, *Middle Age and Aging* (Chicago: University Press, 1968), p. 23.

6. Colin Parkes, *Bereavement: Studies in Grief in Adult Life* (New York: International Universities Press, 1972), p. 536.

7. Naomi Golan, *The Perilous Bridge—Helping Clients Through Mid-Life Transitions* (New York: Free Press, 1986), pp. 96–113.

8. Weenolsen, *Transcendence of Loss*, pp. 60–64.

9. Erich Lindemann, "Symptomatology and Management of Acute Grief," in *American Journal of Psychiatry* 101 (September, 1944), pp. 141–48.

10. Clinebell, "The Five Tasks of Grief," video series, *Growing Through Grief*.

11. Paul Tournier, *Learn To Grow Old* (New York: Harper & Row, 1983), pp. 218–19, 222, 231, 235–36.

Chapter 6: The Pain of Suicide

1. The name and other incidental biographical details have been changed to protect confidentiality.

2. Greg Laurie, *The Final Cry* (Eugene, Oreg.: Harvest House, 1987), pp. 9, 18, 21; Diane Eble, "Too Young To Die," in *Christianity*

Today (March 20, 1987), p. 19; Michael Peck, "Youth Suicide" in *Death Education* 6 (1982), pp. 29–32; Lynne Ann DeSpelder and Albert Lee Strickland, *The Last Dance* (Palo Alto: Mayfield, 1987), p. 421.

3. Anthony J. La Greca, "Suicide: Prevalence, Theories, and Prevention" in *Dying: Facing the Facts* (San Francisco: Hemisphere, 1988), pp. 230–33; Kalish, *Dying, Grief, and Caring Relationships* (Monterey, Calif.: Brooks/Cole, 1985*)*, p. 160; Earl A. Grollman, *Suicide* (Boston: Beacon, 1971), pp. 5–6, 11, 46–47.

4. Kalish, *Death, Grief, and Caring Relationships*, p. 160; Edwin S. Schneidman, *Death: Current Perspectives* (Palo Alto: Mayfield, 1980), pp. 446–65, 520–30; DeSpelder and Strickland, *The Last Dance*, p. 421; Grollman, *Suicide*, pp. 1–14, 43–68.

5. La Greca, *Dying—Facing the Facts*, pp. 237–39.

6. Emile Durkheim, *Suicide* (New York: Free Press, 1951).

7. Laurie, *The Final Cry*, p. 18.

8. Edward F. Ansello, "The Environmental Press Model: A Theoretical Framework for Intervention in Elder Abuse," in *Elder Abuse: Conflict in the Family* (Dover, Mass.: Auburn, 1988), pp. 314–30.

9. Schneidman, *Death: Current Perspectives*, p. 416; La Greca, *Dying—Facing the Facts*, pp. 229–30.

10. B. T. Gates, "Suicide and the Victorian Physicians" in *Journal of the History of the Behavioral Sciences* (1980) 16:164–74.

11. Stephen Levine, *Who Dies?* (New York: Doubleday, 1982), p. 218.

12. Alex D. Pokorny, "Myths About Suicide," in *Death and Dying: Challenge and Change*, ed. Robert Fulton (Reading, Mass.: Addison-Wesley, 1978), pp. 340–46.

13. Robert Kastenbaum, *Death, Society, and Human Experience*, 2d ed. (St. Louis: Mosby, 1981), pp. 239–55.

14. Philippe Aries, *The Hour of Our Death* (New York: Knopf, 1981), p. 44.

15. Grollman, *Suicide: Prevention, Intervention, Postvention*, p. 53.

16. Edgar Draper and Bevan Steadman, "Assessment in Pastoral Care" in *Clinical Handbook of Pastoral Counseling*, ed. R. J. Wicks et. al. (New York: Paulist, 1984), p. 124.

17. Laurie, *The Final Cry*, pp. 15–16.

Chapter 7: The Challenge of Aging

1. John Tierney, "The Aging Body" in *Aging*, 5th ed. (Guilford, Conn.: Duskin Publishing Group, 1987), pp. 42–47.

2. Theodore Seuss Giesel, *You're Only Old Once!* (New York: Random House, 1986), p. 43.

3. *The Gallup Report,* Nos. 201–2. June-July, 1982.

4. Pat Murphy, "Spirituality and Aging: Fostering Spiritual Well Being of an Older Adult" in *Aging Network News* vol. III, no. 8, Dec. 1986, p. 1.

5. Nathan W. Shock, "Human Aging" in *Encyclopaedia Britannica,* 15th ed. (Chicago: Benton Publishers, 1977), 1:305.

6. William Shakespeare, *As You Like It,* Act II, Scene VII, 26–29.

7. Gail Sheehy, *Pathfinders* (New York: William Morrow, 1981), pp. 219–20.

8. Tierney, *Aging,* p. 46.

9. Alan Pardini, "Exercise, Vitality and Aging," in *Aging,* 5th ed. (Guilford, Conn.: Dushkin Publishing, 1987), pp. 55–56, 58, 60.

10. Sharan Merriam and D. Barry Lumsden, "Educational Needs and Interests of Older Learners," in D. Barry Lumsden, ed. *The Older Adult As Learner* (Washington, D.C.: Hemisphere, 1985), pp. 59–60.

11. Barbara F. Okun, *Working with Adults: Individual, Family, and Career Development* (Monterey, Calif.: Brooks/Cole, 1984), pp. 328–29.

12. Lyle D. Schmidt and Gary W. Piggrem, "Counseling the Older Adult Learner," in D. Barry Lumsden, ed. *The Older Adult As Learner* (Washington, D.C.: Hemisphere, 1985), pp. 177, 180, 182, 187.

13. John Naisbitt, *Megatrends—Ten New Directions Transforming Our Lives* (New York: Warner Books, 1982), pp. 16–17.

14. Murray G. Ross, *The University—The Anatomy of Academe* (New York: McGraw-Hill, 1976), pp. 257–58.

15. Mortimer R. Feinberg, *Leavetaking* (New York: Simon & Schuster, 1978), p. 91.

16. Charles M. Sell, *Transition* (Chicago: Moody Press, 1985), p. 219.

17. Nancy K. Schlossberg, *Counseling Adults in Transition* (New York: Springer, 1984), pp. 5–40, 65, 108, 110–12, 169–87.

18. Sheehy, *Pathfinders,* p. 22.

Chapter 8: The Mentoring of Children

1. Hannelore Wass and Charles A. Corr, eds. *Childhood and Death* (Washington, D.C.: Hemisphere, 1984).

2. Watson, *The Pastoral Role in Caring for the Dying and Bereaved,* pp. 31–81.

3. Acts 22:3; 23:16; 26:4–5; Gal. 1:14–16; Phil. 3:5–6.

4. Acts 6:8–8:3; 22:20.

5. Acts 8:3; 9:1–31; 22:3–21; 26:9–21; 2 Cor. 11:32–33; 1 Tim. 1:13.

6. Acts 13:1–21:40; Rom. 16:3–4; 1 Cor. 4:12; 15:31–32; Col. 4:10.

7. Acts 21–28; Phil. 1:12–13; 4:22; 2 Tim. 4. (Paul's conversation with Pudens is not in the Bible but is typical of Paul's missionary effort.)

8. *L.A. Times News Service* for January 20, 1990.

Chapter 9: The Care of Sufferers

1. Peter Carlson, "A Life Without Hope" in *The Washington Post Magazine,* April 26, 1987, pp. 32–35, 44–52.

2. Charles Swindoll, *For Those Who Hurt* (Portland, Oreg.: Multnomah, 1980), p. 4.

3. Mitchell Dahood, *Psalms II* (Garden City, N.Y.: Doubleday, 1968), p. 302.

4. C. R. Figley and H. I. McCubbin, *Stress and the Family,* 2 vols. (New York: Brunner/Mazel, 1983).

5. R. Dayringer, "The Religious Professionals' Contribution to Health Care," *Surgery Annual* 15 (1983), p. 113.

6. William F. Arndt and F. Wilbur Gingrich, *A Greek-English Lexicon of the New Testament* (Chicago: University of Chicago Press, 1957), p. 247.

7. Joseph F. Fichter, *Religion and Pain* (New York: Crossroads, 1981), pp. 91–92.

8. R. C. H. Lenski, *The Interpretation of the Epistle of James* (St. Louis: Augsburg, 1960), p. 660.

For Further Reading

R. C. Atchley, *The Social Forces in Later Life—An Introduction to Social Gerontology* (Belmont, Calif.: Wadsworth, 1980).

H. T. Bryson, *The Reality of Hell and the Goodness of God* and *Leader's Guide* (Wheaton: Tyndale, 1984).

J. Choron, *Death and Western Thought* (New York: Collier, 1963).

W. M. Clements, *Ministry with the Aging* (San Francisco: Harper, 1981).

N. Cousins, *Anatomy of an Illness As Perceived by the Patient* (Toronto: Bantam, 1979).

N. Cousins, *Head First—The Biology of Hope* (New York: Dutton, 1989).

M. Eliade, *Death, Afterlife, and Eschatology* (New York: Harper & Row, 1974).

H. Faber, *Striking Sails—A Pastoral Psychological View of Growing Older in Our Society,* trans. by K. R. Mitchell (Nashville: Abingdon, 1984).

J. H. Fichter, *Religion and Pain—The Spiritual Dimensions of Health Care* (New York: Crossroad, 1981).

R. M. Gray and D. O. Moberg, *The Church and the Older Person* (Grand Rapids: Eerdmans, 1977).

S. Hauerwas, *Suffering Presence—Theological Reflections on Medicine, the Mentally Handicapped, and the Church* (Notre Dame: University Press, 1986).

E. B. Holified, *A History of Pastoral Care in America—From Salvation to Self-Realization* (Nashville: Abingdon, 1983).

P. E. Irion, *The Funeral and the Mourners—Pastoral Care of the Bereaved* (Nashville: Abingdon, 1979).

R. A. Kalish, *Death, Grief, and Caring Relationships* (Monterey, CA: Brooks/Cole, 1985).

H. G. Koenig, et. al., *Religion, Health, and Aging* (New York: Greenwood Press, 1988).

K. Kramer, *The Sacred Art of Dying* (New York: Paulist, 1988).

E. Kubler-Ross, *On Death and Dying* (New York: Macmillan, 1969).

C. S. Lewis, *The Problem of Pain* (New York: Macmillan, 1962).

P. L. McKee, *Philosophical Foundations of Gerontology* (New York: Human Sciences, 1982).

A. Pifer and L. Bronte, *Our Aging Society—Paradox and Promise* (New York: Norton, 1986).

G. Sheehy, *Pathfinders* (New York: Bantam, 1982).

B. S. Siegel, *Love, Medicine & Miracles* (New York: Harper, 1986).

J. Stevens-Long, *Adult Life—Developmental Process* (Mountain View, Calif.: Mayfield, 1988).

P. Tournier, *Learn to Grow Old* (San Francisco: Harper, 1972).

H. Wass, et. al., *Childhood and Death* (Washington, D.C.: Hemisphere, 1984).

Index

185